The Louisiana Capitol

The Louisiana Capitol

Its Art and Architecture

by
VINCENT F. KUBLY

Foreword by Solis Seiferth,
F. A. I. A.

Pelican Publishing Company

GRETNA 1977

Manufactured in the United States of America
Published by Pelican Publishing Company, Inc.
630 Burmaster Street, Gretna, Louisiana 70053
Designed by Barney McKee

Library of Congress Cataloging in Publication Data

Kubly, Vincent F.
  The Louisiana capitol.

  Includes index.
  1. Baton Rouge, La. State Capitol. I. Title.
NA4413.B36K8 725'.11'0976318 76-49889
ISBN 0-88289-082-4

Contents

Bronze relief map of Louisiana. Floor of Memorial Hall.

Foreword

Some months ago Vincent Kubly, young art professor, critic, and author, advised me that he was writing a critical description of Louisiana's State Capitol and requested my cooperation. Impressed by his scholarship and enthusiasm, I readily agreed to lend my assistance. Together we dug through old files and musty boxes for photographs, letters, papers, and whatever exhibits we could locate that might have survived the years of war, the breaking up of partnerships, and a serious lack of both filing personnel and storage facilities.

The building of Louisiana's capitol filled such an important part of my professional life that I find it hard to realize that close to half a century has passed since its accomplishment. People still refer to it affectionately as the "new" capitol—possibly to distinguish it from the castellated Gothic structure that had served this purpose for eight decades—making me wonder if this name will persist in the same way that Parisians still fondly call their oldest bridge the *Pont Neuf*.

In complying with the publisher's request for a brief foreword, I do so humbly in the realization that I am invited as the only surviving member of Weiss, Dreyfous and Seiferth, the architectural partnership that designed, planned, and administered the construction of Louisiana's capitol during 1929 and the years immediately following. It was a team accomplishment, and the credit, including praise and criticism, must be shared with my partners and with the group of young men who worked with us as draftsmen, engineers, superintendents, and others in field and office.

Besides the importance of the project, the time schedule given to us was an almost impossible one, and putting together an organization to accomplish such a task was in itself no small undertaking. I cannot speak too highly of the fine group of young men who worked with us, tackling their tasks with energy and enthusiasm. I hesitate to recall some names at the risk of forgetting others, but I feel I must extend special mention to a few of cherished memory. Among these are Louis Hammett, who, serving as chief draftsman, did outstanding work in coordinating our ideas and efforts while handling a crew of new and unfamiliar draftsmen and maintaining a rush schedule; David Tanet, who was in charge of the preparation of the specifications; and a superb draftsman like Samuel Wellborn, who did much of the fine detailing this building required.

Our young draftsmen, some just out of architectural schools, performed nobly on the capitol and the many other challenging projects in our office at the time. Without files and records at hand, a few names occur to me: Rolfs, Trepagnier, Bodman, Murrell, Perez, Proctor, Raicevich, Von Osthoff, Silverstein, Kenny, and so on until the list includes many of the leading architects of succeeding decades.

Even after the passage of so many years, details of my varied personal labors connected with this project are still vividly recalled. One of my many specific tasks was to search out and edit an appropriate quotation from Louisiana's history and then lay it out and space it as an inscription, to form panels of texture on the two sides of the great entrance portal to the building. This assignment, allowing me to combine my love of lettering, design, and historical research, was a labor of love and a delightful challenge. After these many years, the opening words of this quotation seem almost personal or prophetic, in much the same way as when a medieval artist painted in figures or symbols as a kind of signature to his work. Perhaps I was speaking for myself, along with Robert Livingston, when I laid out the words:

We have lived long but this is the noblest work of our whole lives.

SOLIS SEIFERTH
Fellow
The American Institute
of Architects

Preface

Louisiana's capitol building in Baton Rouge is today little understood or appreciated for its architectural and artistic merits. Its design and decoration represent architectural fashions and intellectual assumptions current around 1930 but already on the verge of obsolescence at that time. Although the building and the ideas it embodies are still very much out of fashion, its historic importance has been underrated to an extreme. It and buildings like it around the country bear significance that has not been widely recognized, and such buildings are worthy of serious study and elucidation.

The Louisiana capitol epitomizes the end of the Beaux-Arts architectural tradition in America, when a number of prominent architects were attempting to update the waning academic tradition by combining conventional elements of classicism with popular imagery of modernism. This attempted synthesis of classicistic and modernistic elements became passé as the esthetic of functionalism and the economic realities of the Depression radically altered the architectural scene. Architectural ornament was abandoned altogether. The sculptors and mural painters who worked on the Louisiana capitol included some of the most prominent artists in their fields at the time, but these men are now largely forgotten and their creations neglected. The involved literary and symbolic content of the capitol's decoration, intended to embody the noblest of human values and aspirations for the instruction and enlightenment of future generations, is largely unintelligible, and few make the effort to decipher the building's message and meaning.

This book intends to recount the story of the capitol's design and construction, to place it in architectural history with reference to the concepts underlying its design, to discuss some of the more important artists involved, and to illustrate and explain the carved and painted details which are not all easily visible on the building itself and are in many cases unintelligible without written explanation.

Interviews with the architects Solis Seiferth and the late F. Julius

Dreyfous were extremely important in the preparation of this material. In addition to valuable ideas and facts supplied to me verbally, they made available their collections of photographs gathered by their firm while the capitol was under construction. One series of these photos documents the construction from the first excavations to the finishing touches, and a sampling of them is included here. Many of the photos were taken in the sculptors' studios, showing the work in various stages of completion from preliminary studies in clay to finished plaster models. These photos of models are important for showing the sculptors' methods and, in some cases, alterations that were made before final solutions were reached. They were taken from advantageous viewpoints under controlled lighting conditions. In most cases it would be difficult or impossible to make equally good photos of the finished works in place on the building, especially where the stone has discolored. For these reasons I have in many cases used these old photos of sculptors' models in place of photos taken from the actual building.

The Baton Rouge *State Times* edition of May 16, 1932, the date of the dedication ceremony, contains many articles on the capitol, some of which were useful to this study. The article "Louisiana's Capitol Adds Monumental Building to Nation's Fine Structures" gives the technical details of construction, while "Construction of Capitol Here Ends Debate Over Moving Government Seat" recounts the political maneuvering involved in getting the new building approved by the state legislature. "Architects Responsible for Form and Execution of Whole Capitol Plan" explains how the firm handled the complex problems of orchestrating the whole process of design and construction. The article "New Capitol Represents Effort to Tell History in Enduring Materials," written by the architect Leon C. Weiss as part of a sculptural synopsis prepared by his firm, is an extremely important source explaining the symbolic scheme of the capitol's form and ornament, and I have quoted liberally from the florid prose of this article. Other articles deal with such topics as the landscaping, the furnishing, the woodwork, the plumbing, the draperies, the wiring, the color scheme of the interior, the methods of stone carving, the bronzework, the mural paintings, and some of the relief sculptures.

The article "The South's New Skyscraper Capitol" in the December, 1932, issue of *Architectural Forum* is the only material on the capitol to appear in a national publication. It contains a good selection of illustrations, floor plans, and a concise text describing the architects' ideas and methods and briefly outlining the symbolism of the major details.

A twenty-six-page document entitled "A Brief Description of Louisiana's New State Capitol," prepared by the architects, discusses the symbolism, materials, and functions of the building. It is especially useful for its description of the interior decor.

The booklet *Louisiana, Its Capitol,* prepared in 1932 by Helen Emmelin Wurzlow, the capitol's official hostess, was intended primarily as a guide for tourists. It gives little information not available elsewhere, does not concern itself much with explanation of the imagery, and contains a couple of minor inaccuracies.

Walter Raymond Agard's book, *The New Architectural Sculpture* (New York, 1935), a survey of the architectural sculpture of the period, includes some useful comments on the Louisiana capitol, which I have quoted.

The October, 1934, issue of *American Architect,* dedicated to the Nebraska capitol, does not deal with the Louisiana capitol but contains an important description and discussion of the building that embodies many of the same ideas as the Louisiana capitol.

The Louisiana Room of the Louisiana State University Library has maintained a file of newspaper clippings on the capitol. Much of that material was irrelevant to the purpose of this study, but it remains an important source for the history of the capitol in the decades after its construction.

I should like to express special appreciation to H. Parrott Bacot, Curator of the Anglo-American Art Museum at Louisiana State University in Baton Rouge, and Mrs. Lawrence T. Lowrey for special assistance in the preparation of this work.

The Louisiana Capitol

I

Huey Long's Monument

The new Louisiana capitol building in Baton Rouge owes its existence and basic format to Huey Long. By 1930 the old neo-Gothic capitol built by the architect James H. Dakin on the banks of the Mississippi in 1847 was functionally obsolete, no longer large enough for the efficient operation of the state government. A new capitol was necessary, and it was Governor Long who took the initiative and used his political power to make the idea a reality in a remarkably short period of time.

Long first expressed his hope of constructing a new capitol in a speech while campaigning for governor in 1927. Elected the next year, he began to promote the project vigorously. In his efforts to convince the public and the legislature that a new state house was necessary, he based his arguments on the savings he believed would accrue through the state's increased efficiency of operation in a more modern structure.[1] However, it is obvious that Long, with a sense of history and posterity, was motivated largely by the desire to build a monument. There are many sacrifices of strict economy and efficiency in the new capitol—wasted space, relief sculptures, statues, mural paintings, elaborate bronzework, and costly marble decoration. He chose the format of a tall tower, which is inefficient due to the relatively small amount of office space on each floor and the large amount of space taken up by elevator shafts.[2] Much of the base is occupied by the Memorial Hall, a large two-story public space decorated with mural paintings, reliefs, statues, and richly veined marble but lacking a specific function. The elaborate program of sculptural ornament decorating the exterior certainly has nothing to do with economy or efficiency. There were many sacrifices of strict expediency in order to enhance the building's symbolic and monumental aspects, and it is these sacrifices and luxuries that give the capitol its architectural distinction and historic importance.

Long made the first move toward actual construction in January, 1930,

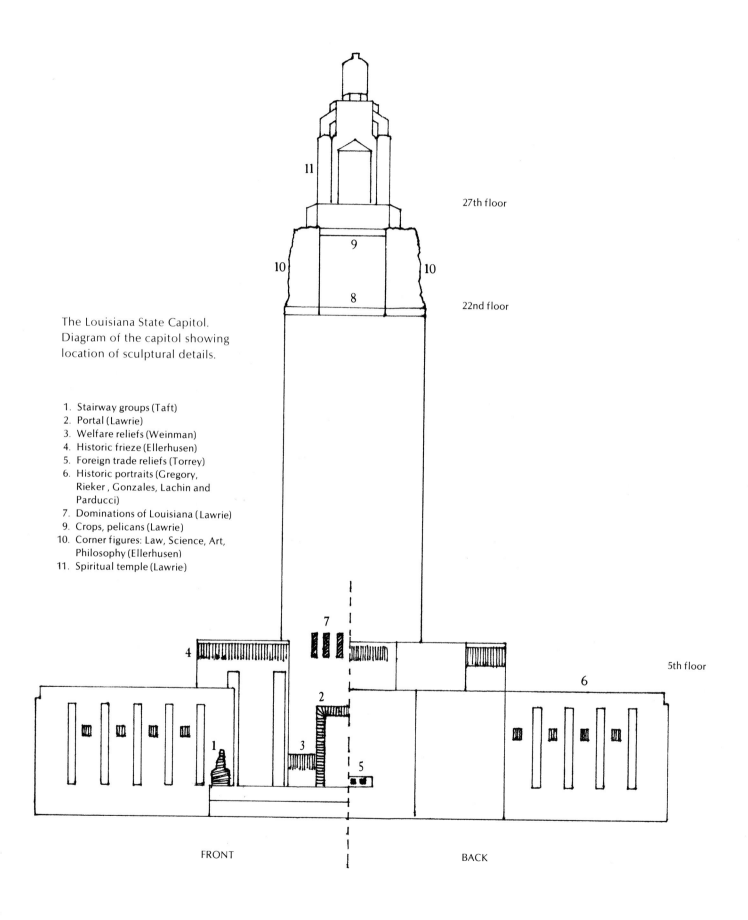

The Louisiana State Capitol.
Diagram of the capitol showing
location of sculptural details.

1. Stairway groups (Taft)
2. Portal (Lawrie)
3. Welfare reliefs (Weinman)
4. Historic frieze (Ellerhusen)
5. Foreign trade reliefs (Torrey)
6. Historic portraits (Gregory,
   Rieker , Gonzales, Lachin and
   Parducci)
7. Dominations of Louisiana (Lawrie)
9. Crops, pelicans (Lawrie)
10. Corner figures: Law, Science, Art,
    Philosophy (Ellerhusen)
11. Spiritual temple (Lawrie)

27th floor

22nd floor

5th floor

FRONT

BACK

when he approached the State Board of Liquidation for five thousand dollars to employ the New Orleans architectural firm of Weiss, Dreyfous, and Seiferth to draw up a set of plans.[3] The architects concurred with Long's decision to build a tower. After making an extensive study of other state capitols, they were especially impressed by the Nebraska capitol in Lincoln, designed by Bertram Grosvenor Goodhue in 1920 and under construction until 1934. Inspired by Goodhue's example, they chose to abandon the " 'rotunda-dome-and-wing' type of capitol," which they considered to be outmoded, in favor of a "tower type of building with a broad and dignified base."[4]

Other than specifying that he wanted a tower, Huey Long did not intervene in the design of the capitol. He trusted the architects and gave them a free hand to work out the specifics. Architects Leon C. Weiss and Solis Seiferth studied the history and animal and plant life of Louisiana in order to determine the symbolism of the sculptured details, which Weiss outlined in a written synopsis. Working with the architects, the New Orleans sculptor John Lachin (who also executed some of the portraits on the Senate and House wings) constructed a large plaster scale

An early conception of the capitol.

A later, modified sketch of the proposed capitol.

The capitol under construction on July 3, 1931, viewed from the south.

The capitol under construction on August 1, 1931, viewed from the northwest.

The capitol under construction on August 1, 1931, viewed from the south.

The capitol under construction on August 8, 1931, viewed from the south.

The capitol under construction on August 15, 1931, viewed from the northwest.

model so that the massing and detailing of the building could be studied. The architects took on many extra draftsmen to make working drawings that delineated the details down to the furniture, lighting fixtures, and doorknobs. Preliminary sketches were submitted on March 1, and complete plans and specifications were ready for bidders by early November, 1930.[5]

The project encountered considerable difficulty during the 1930 legislative session, but Huey Long was finally able to impose his will on the legislators. During the regular session the proposal failed to muster support, even from the Baton Rouge delegates to the House. Not long before, an office building which would have cost considerably less than a new capitol had been voted down. Long's overwhelming victory in the September, 1930, U.S. Senatorial election demonstrated his popularity and strengthened his hand in state politics. In a special session of the legislature the constitutional amendment necessary for the construction of a new capitol was appended to a $75 million highway construction bill, which came to the floor of the House on September 18. After the first vote fell four short of the necessary two-thirds majority, the Speaker of the House ordered a roll-call vote. This ploy gave Long, who had been standing in the rear of the chamber, some time to change a few legislators' minds. The final count was seventy-one to twenty-three in favor. There was no problem in the Senate, where the bill passed by a margin of twenty-three to five.[6]

Enabling legislation, requiring only a simple majority vote, established a building commission to oversee the project, which proceeded rapidly from then on. On October 3 the commission settled on the exact site for the building and ordered the detailed working plans. The citizens of the state approved the constitutional amendment by a ratio of fourteen to one in the election of November 4. Six days later the completed plans and specifications were submitted to the bidders. A month later, on December 10, the contract was awarded to the George A. Fuller Company of Washington, D.C., and construction was begun on the 16th.

The Fuller Company was well suited to the task, being experienced in the construction of large public buildings, skyscrapers, and monuments. Among the more important buildings they had erected were the Flatiron Building, one of New York's first skyscrapers; the Lincoln Memorial and National Cathedral of Saints Peter and Paul in Washington; and the state capitol of West Virginia in Charleston.[7]

Construction of Louisiana's new capitol took a little over a year to complete. A spur of the Yazoo and Mississippi Valley Railroad was built to the site to facilitate the delivery of the 2500 carloads of necessary materials, including 200 carloads of limestone, 50 of marble, 26 of granite, 285 of sand, 240 of gravel, 190 of cement, 108 of bricks, 500 of tile, 20 of terrazzo, 30 of bronze, 24 of ornamental iron, and 100 of structural and reinforcing steel. The foundation, consisting of 1900 reinforced concrete piles each sixteen inches square, from forty to sixty feet in length, and designed to support a fifty-ton load, was laid between January 19 and March 31, 1931. The steel skeleton, designed to withstand winds of up to 110 miles per hour, was finished by June 26.

With only one sculpture group remaining unfinished, the 34-story, 450-foot Alabama limestone edifice was dedicated in colorful and elaborate ceremonies which coincided with the inauguration of Governor O. K. Allen on May 16, 1932. According to a Baton Rouge *State Times* report, the visitors who had come from all over the state for the inauguration and dedication festivities experienced a feeling "nothing short of astonishment" on seeing the new capitol for the first time.[8] Ironically Huey Long, who had been sworn in as United States Senator on January 25, was unable to attend the ceremonies because of his duties in Washington.

2

Beaux-Arts Modernism

The capitol represents an effort to update and modernize
the tradition of academic architecture, which was based on
the study of antique and renaissance examples. The architects sought
to create a dramatic image of modernity and progress within an architectural tradition that was respectably conservative. Architect Dreyfous
had received much of his training at the University of Pennsylvania under
Paul Cret, a prominent Paris-trained academician who promoted what
he called the "classic modern." The idea was to design buildings that
would reflect their times while also belonging to a long tradition that
would impart an element of timelessness and keep them from becoming
dated. Architect Weiss wrote:

> The capitol is a modern conception, exemplifying the highly developed
> civilization of the era of its creation. It is simple and restrained both in com-
> position and detail, and though its component masses tend upward, in har-
> mony with the towering masses, beyond the bounds of classical constraint,
> there is a conservatism — a harking back to tradition — to the end of avoid-
> ing that ultra-modernism that might well result in its being branded in future
> critical dictum as obsolescent, or decadent, in style.[9]

The link between American public architecture and the traditions of
classical antiquity was established soon after the Revolution, as the Founding Fathers came to identify the new nation with the republican institu-
tions of ancient Rome. Thomas Jefferson's use of a Roman temple from
the first century B.C. (the Maison Carrée in Nimes, France) as a model
for the Virginia state capitol he designed in 1785 established an important
precedent. The Roman revival of the post-Revolutionary period merged
into a revival of ancient Greek styles in the second quarter of the nineteenth century as the democratic tendencies of the Jacksonian era came
to be identified popularly with the democracy of ancient Greece. After
several decades dominated by more picturesque and exotic architectural
styles, the classic ideal again came into vogue in the 1890s, this time in
an especially eclectic variety as taught at the École des Beaux Arts in

Paris, where most of the fashionable American architects of the time studied. The idea of monumental, gleaming white buildings adorned with classically inspired decorative motifs and figure sculpture was popularized throughout America by the Chicago Columbian Exposition of 1893, as the nation displayed its wealth from the Industrial Revolution and celebrated its emergence as a world power. This vision of the classic ideal persisted in America up to the time of the Depression.

The skyscraper tower was a popular futuristic image in the years around 1930. It emerged in the years before World War I, with New York's Woolworth Building (by Cass Gilbert, 1911–1913) one of the best-known early examples. The international competition held in 1922 for the design of the Chicago Tribune Tower (by Hood and Howells, 1922–1925) attracted the attention of many of the world's leading architects to the problem of designing towers and also did much to popularize the tower in the public imagination. Goodhue's Nebraska capitol, under construction through the 1920s, also attracted a good amount of publicity. By the later 1920s the needle-skyscraper, along with such other marvels as the automobile, wireless radio, and the talking movie, came to epitomize the progress of modern civilization in the public mind. In 1928 the designer Paul T. Frankl published *New Dimensions,* a book outlining his proposals for design in an age of material and scientific progress. He believed that the skyscraper was the symbol of American civilization much as the pyramid had been the symbol of Egyptian civilization. He also designed "skyscraper furniture"—chests and cabinets rising in stepped-back vertical forms like skyscrapers. In 1929 Hugh Ferriss published his book *The Metropolis of Tomorrow,* with fantastic sketches of huge cities of monumental towers and ziggurat-type buildings. New York's Chrysler Building (by William van Allen, 1929–1932) and Empire State Building (by Shreve, Lamb, and Harmon, 1930–1931), two of the best-known needle-skyscrapers, were under construction at the same time as the Louisiana capitol.

The effort to update the classical tradition by adapting it to modernistic forms was not successful. Ironically, the architects of the Louisiana capitol accomplished exactly what they were trying to avoid. The application of classically inspired ornament to building types unprecedented in the classical tradition proved to be incongruous and did not gain wide acceptance. In 1930 both the skyscraper tower and classicistic architectural sculpture were on the verge of obsolescence, and the capitol was dated not long after its completion. The future of large-scale architecture was represented by such buildings as New York's McGraw-Hill Building (by Raymond Hood, 1930–1931) and the Philadelphia Saving Fund Society Building (by Howe and Lescaze, 1932), unadorned "functional" skyscrapers abandoning the tower form in favor of the block and slab which provided more usable floor space.

Its rapid stylistic obsolescence does not diminish the historic importance of the Louisiana capitol. It remains one of the best examples of the end of the Beaux-Arts architectural tradition in America.

3

Architecture
as Literature

The architects of the new capitol believed that the building should not only be functional from a strictly utilitarian point of view, but from a symbolic standpoint as well. It had "first, to serve efficiently as a legislative, executive, and judicial meeting place, with offices for government officials, departments, and bureaus; secondly, to serve as a public monument embodying the history, progress, and aspirations of the people of the state."[10]

The functional divisions of the capitol are clearly articulated in its design. The wings of the base contain the two houses of the legislature —the Senate to the west and the House of Representatives to the east. The north side of the base was occupied by executive offices (of the governor, lieutenant governor, and Speaker of the House) on the first floor and by conference and hearing rooms on the second. The third floor is occupied by more offices. The fourth and fifth, occupying the set-back base of the tower, were given over to the judiciary, containing two courtrooms, the law library, and offices for judges and clerks. (The courts have since been removed from the capitol altogether. One of the courtrooms is now the governor's press room; the other is used as office space. The original law library is now the governor's office.) The tower contains the offices of various agencies and bureaus, with the upper floors originally intended for the judiciary. According to the original scheme the two houses, the executive, the courts, and the bureaus each were to occupy visually separate parts of the building.

While articulating the functions of the various branches of government, the form of the capitol is symbolic as well. More simply stated, the base represents the material and the worldly, and the tower symbolizes the spiritual.

This distinctive form, of massive base and towering shaft, loftiness growing out of broad solidity — suggests a dualism of theme which has inspired the sculpture and adornment of the building: the broad, substantial base, expressing the material resources of Louisiana and the historic struggles and

27

achievements of her people, buttressing and sustaining the tower rising majestically toward the Heavens, symbolizing the lofty aims and ambitions of sovereign people, guided and influenced by self-restraint and self-improvement, to realization of higher and loftier spiritual values.[11]

The materialistic theme of the base is expressed further in its ornamentation, which is dedicated to the history and resources of the state. The architects intended

> to express in stone and granite, bronze and marble, and in other enduring materials, the colorful history of this once unbounded dominion, then struggling colony, and now progressive and powerful state; to depict the valorous deeds of its white explorers in their contacts and conflicts with the native tribes; to recount the struggles and sufferings, trials and triumphs, of its hardy pioneers; to record the heroic endeavors, boundless sacrifices, and masterly accomplishments of its patriots, in war and in peace; and by means of the sculptors' and painters' skill to liven and envisage these for the edification and enlightenment of the generations now living and of those yet unborn.[12]

The frieze topping the stepped-back portion of the base depicts many scenes from Louisiana history and life from the earliest French explorations up to the time of the capitol's construction. Twenty-two individuals especially important to the history of the state are represented in portrait panels above the windows of the House and Senate wings. Relief sculptures surrounding the portal illustrate themes of industry and government, while the free-standing Pioneer and Patriot groups stand as sentinels on the steps.

The spiritual imagery of the top of the tower is simpler and more abstract than the material imagery of the base. Colossal corner figures representing Law, Science, Philosophy, and Art provide a transition to the temple structure decorated with celestial symbols and topped off by an aluminum lantern sending forth a beam of light.

Despite the presence of this spiritual imagery, the basic message of the capitol's imagery is one of materialism and progress. Although the capitol's design is intended to symbolize a dualism of the material and the spiritual, the material imagery plays the dominant role. The spiritual is based on and rises from the material, and is thus dependent on it. The base is a monument to Louisiana's material progress up to 1930, while the tower is a reminder of the progress to be made in the future under the guidance of the spiritual. This faith in the progress of human civilization through material prosperity and spiritual aspiration expressed in the building and the architects' writings seems naïvely optimistic, especially when we recall that the building was constructed during the early years of the Great Depression, when the general faith in material progress was badly shaken.

The symbolic program of the capitol is expressed primarily in terms of relief sculpture. The academic tradition placed great emphasis on the "embellishment" of architecture with sculpture and mural painting. The sculptor Lorado Taft, who designed the Pioneer and Patriot groups on the capitol's steps, wrote that architectural sculpture "has been the foundation of great art in all periods."[13] Some of the most prominent architectural sculptors in the country worked on the Louisiana capitol, but their names are now largely forgotten and their works little appreciated. Economic necessity as well as changing tastes rendered the figurative embellishment of buildings obsolete in the early 1930s.

The architects entertained high hopes of illustrating important historical events and noble spiritual values for the "edification and enlightenment" of future generations, but the message has been lost. It proved to be a false assumption that the meaning of the visual images would be self-evident and that people would be able to recognize and understand them. A criticism directed at the Nebraska capitol in 1934 could be applied to the Louisiana capitol as well:

> Thus the architect confused the purity of his new form by using an archaic symbological treatment that is not understandable to more than a handful of people in the United States. The ancient method of using a building as an historical record and as a means of issuing public proclamations by the use of pictorial symbology was rendered useless by the invention of moveable type. Whether that was for good or ill may be debatable; but the fact remains that people learned to read type and not symbols.[14]

Thus the very idea of adorning buildings with symbolic imagery was recognized as obsolescent soon after both of these capitols were finished. Frank Lloyd Wright, as early as 1901, called for the abolition of literature from architecture. Attacking the pseudo classicism of the academic tradition, he repeated the prophecy from Victor Hugo's *Notre Dame* that "The book will kill the edifice."[15]

Whether the sculptured ornament and mural paintings on the Louisiana capitol are understood or not, they do much to enliven a building that would be excessively severe without them. Since many different artists were involved, the overall ensemble is not as harmonious as it might have been. The historian Walter Raymond Agard, comparing the Louisiana capitol to the Nebraska capitol, commented:

> It is an impressive and useful building, but in some respects lacks the aesthetic distinction of its prototype. The modified classicism is less original than Goodhue's conception; and for the decoration too many sculptors of varying ability and technique were invited to contribute to its magnificence, The result is a profusion of detail which detracts from the sober dignity of the essential plan. The building is overdecorated in too many sculptural styles. In spite of interesting and often admirable detail, the diversity of the adornment makes the total effect somewhat pretentious and distracting.[16]

The sculpture of the Nebraska capitol is all by one sculptor, Lee Lawrie, who worked closely with the architect Goodhue over a long period of time. It is simpler and more restrained, better unified, and more closely integrated with the architecture. The Louisiana capitol was done more hurriedly, and shows it. In response to Agard's criticism it may be argued that the various diverse parts are well enough subordinated to the whole so that they do not detract from it or conflict with each other. Indeed the number of artists and the variety of stylistic modes represented in the capitol enhance the building's historical importance as a showpiece of the last phase of the Renaissance tradition in American architecture.

Sculptor Lorado Taft on scaffolding with warrior figure of Patriot group. Plaster model in background.

4

The Artists

The architects selected the artists to carry out the embellishment of the Louisiana capitol on the basis of their reputations in their fields. The sculptors Lorado Taft, Lee Lawrie, Ulric Ellerhusen, and Adolph A. Weinman and the mural painter Jules Guerin were all artists of national prominence employed to do major portions of the building's decor, while a number of reputable local artists from New Orleans were taken on to do some of the less ambitious details. All of the art work was supervised by the architects. Weiss and Seiferth devised the program of symbolism and dictated the subject matter to the artists. The sculptors sent photographs of their work in progress to the architects, who would approve them or suggest changes. In addition, the architects, mostly Mr. Dreyfous, visited the studios to see the evolving models firsthand. The artists remained at the service of the architects, with limited freedom to invent, but their individual styles were not suppressed.

Taft (1860–1936), who did the Pioneer and Patriot groups on the capitol steps, was generally regarded as the dean of American sculpture in his later years. He had received an academic training in Paris during the years 1883–1886, then established himself at the Art Institute in Chicago. He did mostly free-standing figure groups, of which the Fountain of Time in Chicago (1920) is the most ambitious and best known. His book *The History of American Sculpture,* first published in 1903, was the only such history written before Wayne Craven's book of 1968.

Lee Lawrie (1877–1963), who sculptured the architrave around the portal and the temple at the top of the capitol, was, according to Agard, "the foremost architectural sculptor in America."[17] He had received his training from Augustus Saint-Gaudens, who had dominated American sculpture in the 1880s and 1890s. As a youth Lawrie had been employed at the 1893 Chicago Columbian Exposition to execute the designs of other sculptors in plaster for the adornment of fair buildings. From then on he devoted himself exclusively to architectural sculpture, mostly reliefs inspired by the art of ancient Egypt and Mesopotamia. His most important projects include some of the buildings at the U.S. Military

Academy at West Point; the Harkness Memorial Tower at Yale (where he taught from 1908 to 1919); the International Building, RCA Building, and Atlas statue in New York's Rockefeller Center; the Los Angeles Public Library; and the entire sculptural program of the Nebraska capitol.

Ulric Ellerhusen (1879–1957), sculptor of the historical frieze banding the top of the capitol's base and the four allegorical figures on the tower, had taken up sculpture as a student of Taft. He went on to study under Gutzon Borglum, the sculptor of Mount Rushmore, and Karl Bitter, the chief sculptor of the Wisconsin capitol. He was best known for his Pioneer Monument at Harrodsburg, Kentucky; religious sculptures for the

Early model of Pioneer group. Photograph marked by artist in colored pencil.

Church of Heavenly Rest in New York and the University of Chicago Chapel in Chicago; a relief symbolizing atomic energy for the 1933 Chicago Century of Progress Exposition; and the Pioneer statue atop the Oregon state capitol, in addition to his work in Baton Rouge.

Adolph A. Weinman (1870–1952), who did the two relief panels flanking the portal and the statue of Governor Claiborne in Memorial Hall, was a highly respected academic sculptor and president of the Sculptors' Society of America when the capitol was built. Among his major projects are the designs for the 1916 dime and half dollar coins, a pediment for the Wisconsin capitol, the Soldiers and Sailors Monument in Baltimore, and a frieze for the U.S. Supreme Court Building and pediment for the National Archives Building in Washington.

Taft, Lawrie, Ellerhusen, and Weinman were the most prominent of the capitol's sculptors, but a number of less well-known sculptors also contributed their talents. The New Orleans sculptors Angela Gregory, Albert Rieker, Juanita Gonzales, John Lachin, and Rudolph Parducci did the twenty-two portraits of prominent figures from Louisiana history on the

Sculptor Attillio Piccirilli at work on statue of Henry Watkins Allen.

Lorado Taft supervising carving of Patriot group.

Senate and House wings. Miss Gregory had studied under the prominent French sculptor Antoine Bourdelle, and Agard characterized her as "one of Bourdelle's most promising pupils."[18] Lachin also prepared the plaster scale model of the capitol for the architects and, with Parducci, did the decorative plaster work inside the building. Rieker made the statue of Bienville in Memorial Hall in addition to his portrait reliefs. Fred M. Torrey, of Chicago, did the four relief panels on the rear balcony, and Isadore Konti, a New York sculptor, modeled the statue of Governor Nicholls in Memorial Hall.

All of the actual stone carving for the architectural sculpture was done by the artisan C. M. Dodd and a staff of assistants. It was a common practice for academic sculptors, most of whom were not stonecutters, to make models of their projects first in clay then in plaster. The models would then be translated into stone by skilled craftsmen using precision measuring devices to achieve an accurate reproduction. Using air drills and chisels, Dodd and his crew worked directly on the wall of the lower portions of the capitol. The work higher up was carved before being mounted in place.[19]

Models for the capitol's extensive bronzework were executed by the Piccirilli brothers of New York City. These six brothers operated a large sculpture *atelier* concerned largely with the execution of works designed by others. Attillio (1868–1945), one of the brothers to achieve some prominence as a sculptor in his own right, did the statue of Governor Allen in Memorial Hall in addition to his part in the bronzework.

The work of the Piccirillis was directed particularly by Seiferth, who remained in New York City for weeks at a time on several occasions.

Jules Guerin (1866–1946), painter of the two large allegorical murals at the ends of Memorial Hall, was a nationally known painter who had done murals for the old Pennsylvania Station in New York, the Federal Reserve Bank of San Francisco, the Lincoln Memorial in Washington, the Cleveland Railroad Terminal, and the Chicago Civic Opera House, to name a few of his larger projects. Guerin also designed the ceiling of Memorial Hall, which the painters Louis Borgo and Andrew Mackey did under his direction.

Murals for the governor's reception room and two courtrooms were the first important commissions for the New Orleans painter Conrad Albrizio (1894–1973). He had been trained as an architect in New York but turned more to painting after his move to New Orleans in 1921. He studied fresco painting in France and Italy and was to paint many murals around the state after his work at the capitol.[20] He taught at Louisiana State University from 1936 to 1953.

Many artists of national and regional prominence participated in the decoration of the capitol. The fact that their names are now forgotten and their work out of fashion does not diminish the importance of their contributions to the expiring academic tradition which the capitol so perfectly epitomizes.

5

The Steps and Portal

The forty-nine steps of the monumental stairway, made of granite from Minnesota, are inscribed with the names of the mainland states in the order of their admittance to the Union. Alaska and Hawaii, admitted after the capitol was constructed, were added alongside the motto E Pluribus Unum on the top step. In the stairway the architects had two ideas in mind, to express a welcome to visitors from other states and to symbolize the interdependence of the states in the Union.

The blocky piers flanking the stairs are decorated with a frieze based on stylized pelican and lotus motifs. The pelican, Louisiana's state bird, expresses the idea of love for posterity while the lotus, indigenous to the state, is a symbol of fertility and "in a higher sense, immortality."

On the topmost of these piers are the only free-standing sculpture groups of the capitol, Lorado Taft's Pioneers and Patriots, conceived as memorials to the settlers and defenders of Louisiana. The two groups, carved from Indiana limestone, are composed similarly, each with a large central symbolic figure surrounded by a variety of figures representing the people. Architect Weiss explained the significance of the two groups in the following terms:

> The west buttress group, the "Pioneers," is a tribute to the founders of Louisiana, who with fortitude explored and inhabited the valley and over-came the forces of man and nature through the early periods of its development. The French and Spanish explorers and colonists of the seventeenth and eighteenth centuries, the Indians who were the original inhabitants of this region, and the American, who, attracted by the fertility of the land and the advantages of location of this section of the country, came here to found homes and farms and to establish commercial enterprises — to the great soldiery of peace, and to statesmanship.

> The east buttress group, the "Patriots," is a memorial to those Louisianians, of heterogeneous nationalities, who shed their blood in defense of their homes and in the establishment of their liberties; who fought to repel the

Steps.

usurper and the foreign foe; who, under great strategists and leaders, such as Gen. Andrew Jackson, set boldly the name of Louisiana and of New Orleans upon the pages of history, and contributed their portion in accomplishing the solidarity of the Union of American states. And in the group there is expressed the sorrows of war, depicted in the piteous figures of the mother and father, the widow and the orphan, of the armed defender. This group is dedicated to the brave soldiery of war, to militant patriotism.[21]

The Pioneer group is dominated by a large "dreamy-eyed woman" personifying the Spirit of Adventure, who stands atop a pair of iron-bound treasure chests. At her feet the various fruits and vegetables that grow in Louisiana lie on the chest. The figures grouped around the treasure chests and allegorical figure are led by the explorers De Soto and La Salle, representing the Spanish and French who first came to the area. Two missionary priests following these explorers hold an open Bible over the symbolic treasure. The hooded monk behind De Soto represents the Franciscan friars who followed in the wake of the Spanish explorers to convert savage natives to Christianity, while the priest to the rear of La Salle may be a representation of the Jesuit Father Hennepin, who accompanied him on some of his explorations. Behind these figures is a picturesque entourage composed of a frontiersman in buckskins and a coonskin cap, a Spanish conquistador, French settlers, and Indians.

The central figure of the Patriot group is an armored knight standing over the coffin of a fallen hero, which is surrounded by a group of mourners.[22] On the bier are a wreath and a palm, symbols of mourning and sacrifice. The mourners are led by an aged couple and a man holding his hat over his heart, conveying the ideas of bereavement and lamentation quite expressively. The other mourners in the procession are rather stereotyped, less varied than the Pioneers, owing to the nature of the subject.

Agard criticized the picturesqueness of the Pioneer and Patriot groups:

A pioneer woman, heroic in size but sweetly sentimental in her attitude of enraptured dreaming, is surrounded by a number of actual pioneers in smaller scale; similarly the stern mailed warrior representing patriotism stands guard over various types of surging citizens beneath him. There is a wealth of picturesque suggestion in the groups and they are skillfully composed from a romantic point of view, but for an entrance a simpler and more severe treatment would have been wiser.[23]

The theme of Weinman's two relief panels flanking the portal is "the protection and encouragement extended by the sovereign state through its functions to the welfare of its people, this welfare being expressed in its dual phases of material advancement on the one hand and their high aspirations on the other."[24] These panels are especially difficult to decipher, since their meanings are expressed in completely allegorical terms with no specific reference to Louisiana history or life. They are in fact unintelligible without written explanation.

The panel to the left of the portal represents the theme "Government based on Law, Order, and Justice fostering the Higher Aspirations of the

The Patriots, by Lorado Taft. East stairway buttress.

Patriots. Detail.

The Pioneers, by Lorado Taft. West stairway buttress.

Pioneers. Detail.

People." Governmental Authority, a muscular and heroic bearded male figure seated under a tree, dominates the group of figures. His left arm holds a bundle of fasces, a traditional symbol of governmental power, while his right arm rests on a book, symbolizing the Law. Accompanying this Zeus-like figure are Peaceful Enforcement of Order, a helmeted figure holding a sheathed sword, and the Genius of Justice, a young boy with a pair of balances. Leading the procession from the left is Education,

Model for old couple in Patriot group.

shown as a female figure in an academic robe bearing a lamp of learning, guiding a young man and woman in quest of knowledge. Science follows the Education group, carrying a globe and compass symbolizing knowledge of the world while trampling the Demon of Ignorance and Superstition beneath his feet. The next figure to the left is Religion, a draped and hooded female "instructing a young boy in the life celestial." She does not bear any symbolic objects that would identify her as a religious figure. The last figure is a lone seminude female crowned with a laurel wreath and playing a harp, a personification of Art.

The figures in the corresponding relief panel to the right are arranged similarly to those on the left, so that the two together form a symmetrical arrangement. The subject is "The Spirit of Liberty and Peace Furthering the Material Welfare of the People." The Spirit, described as a "beautiful female figure of heroic proportions," sits beneath a fruit tree holding the torch of liberty in one hand and the olive branch of peace in the other. She is accompanied by the Genius of Abundance, a youth bearing a horn of plenty. Agriculture, a bearded male figure carrying a sheaf of grain on his shoulder, leads the procession from the right. After him is Lumbering, leaning on an axe and resting one foot on a stump. The handicrafts Pottery and Weaving follow, bearing a large vase and a cotton blossom and distaff. With three unidentified background figures disregarded, the group terminates with the ancient god Hermes or Mercury appearing as a personification of Commerce. The messenger of the gods wears his winged cap and sandals, bears his traditional caduceus, and leans on a rudder referring to shipping.

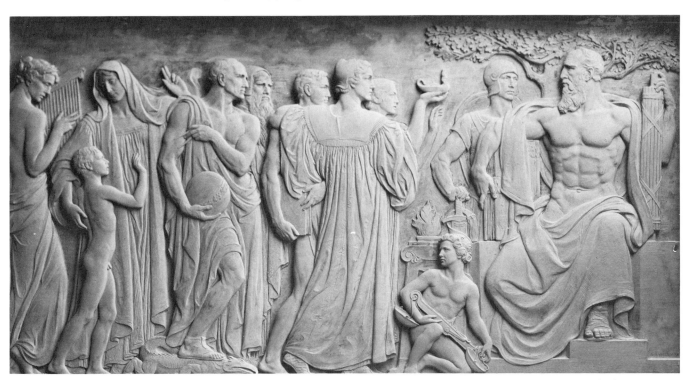

Government Based on Law, Order, and Justice Fostering the Higher Aspirations of the People. Relief panel to left of portal, by Adolph A. Weinman.

The Spirit of Liberty and Peace Furthering the Material Welfare of the People.
Relief panel to right of portal, by Adolph A. Weinman.

Weinman's two panels are inspired by Roman relief sculpture of the first century A.D. The anatomy and poses of the figures are free and natural, and their drapery hangs in loose folds. Within the limitations of the bas-relief technique, there is a convincing illusion of depth. The figures possess corporeal volume and inhabit a space in which they can move with ease. The surfaces are subtly modulated, and the play of light and shadow enhances the illusion of the third dimension.

All of this is in direct contrast with Lee Lawrie's style as seen in the architrave surrounding the portal. Lawrie sought to decorate a flat architectural surface rather than to create naturalistic illusions of volume, space, and light. His art is more two-dimensional than Weinman's, carved in lower relief, with little illusion of volume. The surface is less "broken" by contrasts of light and shadow. Lawrie's sources of inspiration were ancient Egypt and Mesopotamia rather than Rome. Most conspicuous is the stylization of his figures, which is based on ancient Near Eastern conventions intended to show the figure as completely as possible on a flat surface. His figures cutting cane, picking cotton, fishing, logging, harvesting, and building are all posed similarly with the torso seen from the front, the arms, legs, and head in profile, and one foot placed ahead of the other. The contours of the figures are stiff and angular, imparting a rigidity common to Egyptian art. The figures are flattened into a very shallow space, pressed against an imaginary foreground surface. The various parts are placed parallel to the picture surface and arranged so as not to overlap each other. The modeling of the figures is incised and linear, which only enhances the flatness of their cut-out shapes. There are

Central section of main (south) façade, showing portal, relief panels, inscription, and part of frieze.

Model of portal, with reliefs illustrating the industries and resources of Louisiana, by Lee Lawrie.

The Louisiana state seal, with eagles symbolizing the federal government. Top of portal.

Education, science, and the arts. Detail of portal, top left.

Louisiana state motto, with figures representing the law. Top of portal, central section.

Religion, music, drama. Detail of portal, top right.

Communication. Detail of portal, top right.

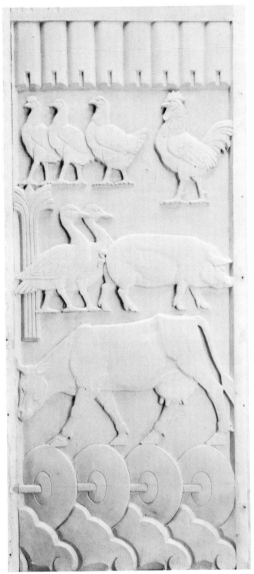

Livestock. Detail of portal, right side.

Agriculture, trucking. Detail of portal, right side.

Shipping. Detail of portal, right side.

River transportation, railroad. Detail of portal, right side.

Fishing. Detail of portal, right side.

Cotton. Detail of portal, right side.

Engineering, petroleum. Detail of portal, left side.

Building. Detail of portal, left side.

Lumbering, forestry. Detail of portal, left side.

Manufacturing, trapping. Detail of portal, left side.

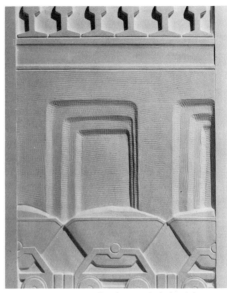

Mining. Detail of portal, left side.

Sugarcane. Detail of portal, left side.

49

only two planes in Lawrie's relief style, foreground and background, with no graduation or transition between them. As artificial as Lawrie's style is, it is imposing and forceful, and well suited to the decoration of architecture.

Lawrie's portal reliefs are dedicated to the theme of Louisiana's economy and resources. The vertical sections of the architrave illustrate scenes of industry and agriculture, with five major scenes on each side separated by smaller representations. To the left are the industries of sugar, petrochemicals, lumbering, building, and engineering, represented by a man cutting cane, a refinery, a man sawing a log, a city skyline, and a construction worker. Between these major scenes are, from the bottom, a mine, animal pelts, leaves, derricks, and coins representing mineral wealth, fur trapping, forestry, oil, and banking. To the right are the industries of cotton, fishing, shipping, farming, and livestock, represented by a cotton picker, a pair of fishermen hauling in a net, a large ship, a harvester with a scythe, and a group of barnyard animals and fowl. Separating these panels are the various modes of transportation represented by a train, a riverboat, and a truck, while a harrow and sheaves refer to planting and harvesting in connection with the agricultural scenes of the upper right.

The horizontal top section of the architrave illustrates themes of "information and craftsmanship": education, science, the arts, law, religion, and communication. From the left, a teacher pointing at a globe instructs a group of three pupils, a scientist peers through a microscope, and a sculptor carves a capital. In the center are five frontally seated judges, the middle one holding a pair of balances. Moving to the right, there is a cathedral-like building with symbols representing the Catholic, Protestant, and Jewish faiths, then a lyre and mask symbolizing music and drama. At the far right are a telegraph operator, a radio announcer, and a printer representing the communications media.

Crowning the portal is the Louisiana state seal, the pelican piercing its breast to nourish its young with its own blood, set between two eagles in profile which represent the protective powers of the federal government. Immediately below the seal is the state motto: Union, Justice, Confidence.

The inscriptions on either side of the portal are quoted from Robert R. Livingston, the American ambassador who negotiated the purchase of the Louisiana territory from France:

> We have lived long, but this is the noblest work of our whole lives. It will transform vast solitudes into thriving districts. The United States take rank today among the first powers of the world.
> The instruments which we have just signed will cause no tears to be shed; they prepare ages of happiness for innumerable generations of human creatures.
>
> Robert R. Livingston, May 3, 1803, after the signing of the treaty purchasing Louisiana from France.

Above the portal and serving as bases for the vertical shafts on the front of the tower are six figures by Lawrie representing the nations that have ruled Louisiana through history. These figures appear to grow out of the architecture, and their garments dissolve into architectural flutings which are adorned with appropriate coats of arms. The end figures, placed in profile facing each other, are Indians representing the original inhabitants. Their "coats of arms" were obviously creations of the sculptor. The other four figures face frontally. From the left, a female figure representing the Spanish holds a model of the Cabildo, the seat of the Spanish regime in Louisiana. The next figure, a female holding an olive branch and arrows, personifies the United States, while a simply dressed female holding a cotton plant stands for the Confederacy. France is represented by a male figure holding a fleur-de-lis and a spyglass and document referring to the early exploration and settlement.

Between these figures are five relief panels illustrating "those ideals and virtues which underlie civilization and the progress of nations under whatever flag or dominance may prevail." Industry is represented by a beehive, Justice by a pair of balances, Liberty by a torch and wreath, Power by a fasces and sword, and Learning by a book and lamp.

Main portal, with Dominations of Louisiana above.

Indian.
Base of tower, above portal, left.

Spain.
Base of tower, above portal.

The United States.
Base of tower, above portal.

The Confederacy.
Base of tower, above portal.

France.
Base of tower, above portal.

Indian.
Base of tower, above portal, right.

Industry. Base of tower, above portal.

Liberty. Base of tower, above portal.

Power. Base of tower, above portal.

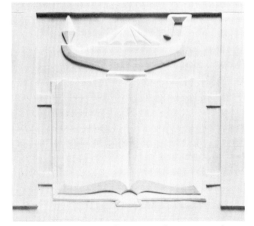

Learning. Base of tower, above portal.

The Dominations of Louisiana.

6

The Wings

Between the pilasters surrounding the Senate and House wings are twenty-two square plaques bearing profile portraits of historic personages especially important to Louisiana's development. Above the portraits are relief panels bearing two alternating designs relating to the theme of fertility. The one symbolizes "the beneficence of the great orb of heat and light in the productive yield of the soil," the other "the rain and water, showing at each side floral volutes and water plants." These are outstanding examples of Art Deco. The tops of the pilasters bear stylized lotus motifs, also symbolizing fertility.

The models for the portraits were made by New Orleans sculptors, but certain aspects of their design such as scale, positioning, and depth of relief were specified by the architects so that the portraits would harmonize with each other. Angela Gregory, assigned eight of the twenty-two heads, was given first choice and selected those figures whose lives she found the most interesting: White, Jefferson, Benjamin, Touro, Tulane, Gottschalk, Audubon, and Gayarré. Albert Rieker modeled the portraits of Livingston, Claiborne, La Salle, Iberville, Beauregard, and Zachary Taylor. John Lachin and Rudolph Parducci, working together, are responsible for Bienville, De Soto, Jackson, Allen, McDonogh, and Poydras. Juanita Gonzales did Governor Nicholls and Richard Taylor.

Beginning from the left, facing the front of the capitol, and proceeding counterclockwise around the building, the historic figures are:

Edward Livingston (1764–1836). Came to Louisiana in 1803 after serving as congressman and mayor of New York City; was aide to Jackson at the Battle of New Orleans; elected to Louisiana legislature in 1820 and to Congress in 1822; largely responsible for the Civil Code of Louisiana, drafted in 1823–1824; elected to U.S. Senate in 1829; secretary of state and minister to France under President Jackson; internationally known as lawyer; brother of Robert Livingston, who negotiated the Louisiana Purchase.

William Charles Cole Claiborne (1775–1817). The first governor of Louisiana as U.S. territory, then state 1804–1816.

Portraits above windows, north side, House wing.

Edward Livingston

William C. C. Claiborne

Sieur de Bienville

Sieur de La Salle

Hernando de Soto

Sieur d'Iberville

Andrew Jackson

Henry Watkins Allen

Edward Douglass White

Thomas Jefferson

Judah P. Benjamin

Richard Taylor

Francis T. Nicholls

P. G. T. Beauregard

Zachary Taylor

John McDonogh

Julien Poydras

Judah Touro

Paul Tulane

Louis Moreau Gottschalk

John James Audubon

Jean Baptiste Le Moyne, Sieur de Bienville (1680–1768). French explorer and colonizer, known as the "Father of Louisiana"; explored Gulf Coast and lower Mississippi valley with his brother Iberville in 1699; governor of Louisiana territory 1701–1713, 1718–1725, 1733–1743; founded New Orleans in 1718.

Rene Robert Cavalier, Sieur de La Salle (1643–1687). French trader and explorer; navigated down Mississippi River to Gulf of Mexico in 1682; claimed the river basin for France; named the territory Louisiana; made unsuccessful attempt to establish a colony in Louisiana in 1684.

Hernando de Soto (1496–1542). Spanish conquistador; came to America seeking fortune; discovered Mississippi River in 1541.

Charles Gayarre

Pierre Le Moyne, Sieur d'Iberville (1661–1706). French Canadian naval hero for victories over the British; was sent to explore and colonize the territory claimed by La Salle for France; explored Gulf Coast and lower Mississippi valley; made treaties with Indians; founded Biloxi and Mobile 1698–1702; first governor; known as the "Founder of Louisiana."

Andrew Jackson (1767–1845). From Tennessee; was general who successfully defended Louisiana against the British in the Battle of New Orleans 1814–1815; U.S. President, 1829–1837.

Henry Watkins Allen (1820–1866). Confederate governor of Louisiana 1864–1865; brigadier general in Confederate army; exiled to Mexico after Civil War.

Edward Douglass White (1845–1921). Justice of Louisiana Supreme Court 1878–1891; U.S. senator 1891–1894; chief justice of U.S. Supreme Court 1910–1921.

Thomas Jefferson (1743–1826). American revolutionary leader and third President 1796–1809; purchased Louisiana from France 1803.

Judah P. Benjamin (1811–1884). U.S. senator from Louisiana 1852–1860; attorney general, secretary of war, and secretary of Confederate States of America; known as the "Brains of the Confederacy"; exiled to England after the Civil War.

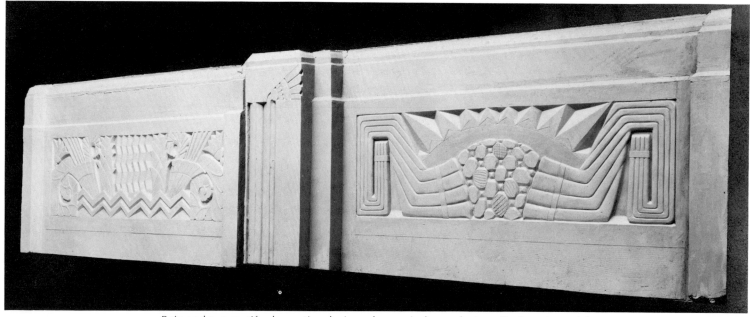

Rain and sun motifs, decorative designs above windows of wings. Sculptor's model.

Richard Taylor (1826–1879). Louisiana state senator 1845–1861; commander of Louisiana forces in Civil War; son of Zachary Taylor.

Francis T. Nicholls (1834–1912). Brigadier general in Confederate army; first post-Reconstruction Democrat governor of state; ended carpetbag rule; governor of Louisiana 1876–1880, 1888–1892; chief justice of Louisiana Supreme Court 1892–1904; associate justice to 1911.

Pierre Gustave Toutant Beauregard (1818–1893). Confederate general, was adjutant general of Louisiana after the Civil War.

Zachary Taylor (1784–1850). U.S. general; hero of the Mexican War; U.S. President 1849–1850; lived in Baton Rouge from 1840.

John McDonogh (1779–1850). New Orleans philanthropist; left money to the city for education of the poor; established asylum and free schools.

Julien Poydras (1740–1824). Poet, philanthropist, and political leader; elected to Congress in 1809; was president of Louisiana's first constitutional convention; gave money for education and charity, donating much of his fortune to Charity Hospital.

Judah Touro (1775–1854). Wealthy merchant and philanthropist; established synagogue; infirmary, and almshouse in New Orleans.

Paul Tulane (1801–1887). Prosperous New Orleans merchant; founded Tulane University.

Louis Moreau Gottschalk (1829–1869). Born in New Orleans; became composer and concert pianist of international reputation; based many of his compositons on Louisana plantation songs.

John James Audubon (1780–1851). Naturalist and illustrator; came from France in 1788; wandered through America studying and drawing birds and wildlife; worked and lived in Louisiana 1820–1826.

Charles Gayarré (1805–1898). Most important historian of Louisiana; published four-volume history of the state between 1854 and 1866, plus many articles and shorter works.

The small balcony on the north or rear side of the capitol, off of the room which was originally the governor's office, bears four relief panels by Fred M. Torrey illustrating the regions of the world most important to the overseas commerce of Louisiana: the Orient, Latin America, the West Indies, and Europe. Each panel is a pastiche of images associated with the life, culture, and production of the region rather than a coherent scene. The Orient relief, described as expressing "all the mysticism of the East," includes camels and an elephant along with human coolies bearing burdens on their backs, bales of some unspecified product, and a background with a smoking volcano and the rigging of a pair of Chinese junks. The Latin America scene depicts a peasant leading a donkey and bearing a basket of bananas on his head, a woman with a jar, a stack of lumber, a Mayan pyramid, and a banana boat. The West Indies scene is set against the fortifications of Havana harbor, with a group of rather athletic-looking peasants, their animals, and their crops of tobacco, sugar, and fruits. Europe is represented by four female figures bearing luxurious artifacts of jewelry, textiles, pottery, and art, with an ocean liner in the background.

Allegories depicting overseas commerce, on north balcony.

Orient.

Latin America.

West Indies.

Europe.

The cornerstone, at the southwest corner of the base, is inscribed on one side with the state seal and the motto We Live for Those We Love, and on the other side with the names of the politicians and architects who built the capitol as well as the date of dedication. Inside the stone is a sealed copper box containing documents relating to the erection of the building: photographs of state officers; names of architects, contractors, and field men; copies of relevant legal documents and legislative acts; a set of specifications; a map of the grounds; an edition of the Baton Rouge *State Times* with stories on the statewide capitol referendum and the awarding of contracts; and copies of Louisiana newspapers (the *Morning Advocate* from Baton Rouge; the *Times-Picayune, Daily States,* and *Item Tribune* from New Orleans; and the *Shreveport Times)* from the day the cornerstone was laid, May 7, 1931.

Cornerstone, southwest corner of base.

ALBRIZIO FRESCO MURALS

Six fresco murals by Louisiana artist Conrad Albrizio once decorated the Louisiana capitol. Only one remains today. Preliminary color sketches of the murals by the artist, however, have been preserved and are reproduced in this color section. Sketches of the four studies for the governor's reception room are now in the collection of the Anglo-American Art Museum, Louisiana State University, Baton Rouge. Sketches of the two studies for the courtrooms are owned by Mrs. Lawrence T. Lowrey of Baton Rouge. Shown above is Old Plantation Life in Louisiana (now destroyed), originally on the east wall of the governor's reception room.

"And the Lord commanded me to teach you statutes and judgments that ye might do these"
(Deuteronomy 4:14). Sketch of mural (now destroyed) in the court of appeals.

"That judgment shall return unto righteousness and all the upright in heart shall follow it" (Psalms 94:15). Sketch of mural originally located in the supreme court room. The mural now decorates the governor's press room on the fourth floor.

CAPITOL SENATE CHAMBER
Architects' rendering,
executed prior to construction

Trucking Cotton and Cutting Sugarcane. Sketch of the mural (now destroyed) on the south wall of the governor's reception room.

Allegory of Louisiana. Sketch of the mural (now destroyed) on the north wall of the governor's reception room.

Industrial Louisiana. Sketch of the mural (now destroyed) on the west wall of the governor's reception room.

7

The Frieze:
Louisiana
History and Life

Ulric Ellerhusen's frieze around the top of the capitol's base, at the fifth-floor level, illustrates various aspects of Louisiana history and life. It exists in five sections, each devoted to a different facet of the state's evolution. The two on the front of the building show important historic incidents from the first European explorations up to the War of 1812 and the Battle of New Orleans. The section to the left, depicting themes of exploration, settlement, and government, emphasizes the more peaceful side of Louisiana's early evolution, while the subject matter to the right is generally more violent and tragic, including a funeral, treaties with Indians, a massacre, a revolt, and a war. The section on the west side wall depicts Louisiana's participation in wars subsequent to the War of 1812, and the corresponding reliefs on the opposite wall depict typical peacetime occupations and activities of Louisianians. The short section of frieze on the north wall illustrates the evolution of Louisiana's system of law.

These reliefs contain a wealth of interesting and picturesque detail, but their rather unfortunate placement at such a height makes it difficult for one to discern the individual details and to read the whole. With the Senate and House wings extending out beneath them, those on the west and east sides are especially difficult to see from the ground. The frieze is repeated in smaller scale and in slightly altered format as a cornice inside Memorial Hall, but owing to the height of its placement and the dimness of the lighting it is also hard to see.

Ellerhusen's style bears many similarities with Lawrie's, but is generally more relaxed and natural, avoiding Lawrie's Egyptian mannerisms. It is flat and linear, with little feeling for roundness or gradation of modeling. Spatial transition is abrupt, with figures filling most of the foreground plane and background details on a much smaller scale crowded into the spaces between them. The figures are generally placed in profile or frontal positions for clarity, but their expressions, poses, and gestures are natural in contrast to Lawrie's grim and straining figures.

The left front section of frieze reads in chronological sequence from right to left, beginning with the early French explorations of the Mississippi River and the Gulf Coast area. The first scene shows Robert de La Salle discovering the mouth of the Mississippi, which he reached on April 7, 1682, after navigating downstream from the north. In a ceremony two days later he claimed the river basin for the French crown and named the territory "Louisiana" in honor of Louis XIV. He points dramatically with his sword while his partner Henri de Tonti and other members of the expedition kneel before him. Behind him, in a short section around the corner near the portal, are a priest and two Indians who belonged to the entourage. The scene immediately to the left depicts the Le Moyne brothers, Iberville and Bienville, on Ship Island, their base for exploration of the Gulf Coast and lower Mississippi valley, in February, 1699. Iberville, the elder brother and commander of the expedition, stands holding a spyglass, while his ship *Badine* may be seen at anchor in the background.

The next few scenes represent the early efforts to settle and develop the Louisiana territory. A pioneer with an axe builds a log cabin, with his wife and child looking on. The gentleman to the left of the pioneer is probably meant to be Antoine Crozat, who attempted unsuccessfully to develop the agriculture and commerce of Louisiana for profit in the years after 1712 but remains important for being the first to promote the settlement and economic development of the region. To the left of him are a trapper and a group of farmers. Next is Bienville with the engineer Adrien de Pauger planning the city of New Orleans in 1721. He holds a map clearly showing the crescent bend in the Mississippi River which he had chosen as the site of his capital and had begun to settle three years earlier. The next group relates the story of the "casket girls," respectable young ladies sent from France in 1727 to find husbands in the colony. Named for the small trunks in which they carried their belongings, the girls are shown in fashionable Parisian dress being received by the Ursuline nuns, who housed them in their convent until they married. These nuns, members of the first religious order in Louisiana, are accompanied by two of the children they cared for in their orphanage. (Ellerhusen used photographs of architect Seiferth's son Solis, Jr., and architect Dreyfous's daughter Carol as models for these children.)

Proceeding leftward, the subject matter changes from themes of settlement and development to that of sovereignty. Bienville appears once more, this time in his capacity as royal French governor of Louisiana, which office he held on and off for most of the period between 1701 and 1743. More than any one individual he personifies the government of Louisiana as a French colony. The next scene shows Bernardo de Galvez, not the first but one of the more colorful and important Spanish governors, presenting his credentials to an assembly of citizens in New Orleans's Place d'Armes (Jackson Square). Then there is the transfer of sovereignty from Spain back to France, which was negotiated in 1800 but not officially consummated until November 30, 1803. A Spanish official, probably meant to be Governor Salcedo, hands the New Orleans city keys to the prefect Laussat, who took over for France although the sale of Louisiana to the United States had already been arranged on April 30. The Louisiana Purchase is shown in the next scene. President Jefferson's special envoy James Monroe stands with the French foreign minister Talleyrand before the seated figure of Robert Livingston, the American ambassador. Napoleon is cleverly included as a bust in the background. The transfer of Louisiana from France to the United States took place on December 20, 1803, three weeks after the transfer from Spain to France. This section of frieze concludes around the corner on the west wall with William C. C. Claiborne, the first American governor, presiding over a flag-raising ceremony.

The scenes of the east front section of frieze proceed in historical sequence from left to right, beginning on the inside corner with the burial of the Spanish explorer De Soto in the Mississippi River in 1542. He and his group were among the first Europeans to explore the territory later known as Louisiana, and he is popularly credited with the discovery of the Mississippi River although others such as Cabeza de Vaca and Alvarez de Pineda got there before him. After his death of a fever, his followers buried him secretly in the river at night so that local Indians would not know. The first systematic exploration of the Mississippi was not until well over a century later, when Father Jacques Marquette and Louis Joliet navigated downstream as far as the mouth of the Arkansas River in 1663. They are shown in the next scene receiving a peace pipe from an Indian chief.

The theme of relations with Indians continues in the next three episodes. The first two are from Iberville and Bienville's expedition of 1699. Iberville sits with the chief of the Houmas Indians of the Pointe Coupee region before a totem pole adorned with votive animal and fish heads. This is the *baton rouge* (red pole or red stick) which Iberville had noted on his way upstream, and which later gave its name to the future capital city. To the right Bienville receives Tonti's letter to La Salle from the chief of the Mougoulachas or Bayou Goula Indians. Tonti had left this letter with the chief in 1685, when La Salle had failed to meet him to establish a settlement. Bienville, fourteen years later, was the next Frenchman to arrive, and the chief gave the letter to him, verifying that the river the Le Moynes were exploring was the same one that La Salle had claimed for France. The next scene shows the first outbreak of Indian trouble in the region, the Natchez massacre of November 26, 1729. Resisting expropriation of their land, the Natchez Indians went on the warpath and annihilated a French settlement of about three hundred, only to be wiped out by French retaliation two years later. Chief Great Sun watches the violence, smoking a pipe.

The next scene commemorates the arrival in Louisiana of the Acadians,

Bienville as governor, the arrival of the Casket Girls, Bienville planning the city of New Orleans, early settlers, pioneer family, Iberville and Bienville on Ship Island, and La Salle and Tonti at the mouth of the Mississippi River. Front wall, left.

Governor William C. C. Claiborne raising the American flag, the Louisiana Purchase, the transfer of Louisiana from Spain to France, Governor Bernardo de Gálvez presenting his credentials, Bienville as governor, and the arrival of the casket girls. Front wall, left and around corner onto west wall. Clay model in rough state.

La Salle claiming the Mississippi Valley for France. Front wall, left, inside corner.

The raising of the American flag, the Louisiana Purchase, and the transfer of Louisiana to France. Model in more highly finished state.

The burial of De Soto, Marquette and Joliet with Indian chief, Iberville with Houmas chief, Bienville receiving Tonti's letter from Mougoulachas chief, the Natchez massacre, the arrival of the Acadians, and the execution of the leaders of the Revolt of 1768. Front wall, right.

The burial of De Soto. Front wall, right, inside corner.

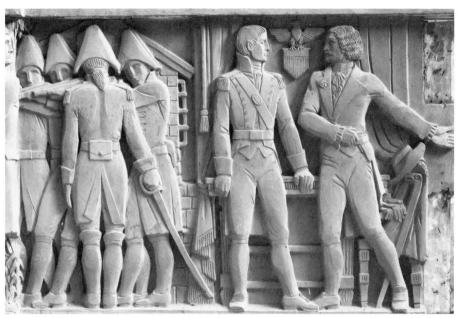

The execution of the rebels of 1768, Jean Lafitte offering his services to Governor Claiborne. Front wall, right.

The Battle of New Orleans. Around corner on east wall.

The Battle of New Orleans. Front wall, right.

who had been expelled from Nova Scotia by the English rulers of Canada in the early 1760s. The new settlers are welcomed by a Creole gentleman and a mammy with loaves of bread, while children play in the foreground. (As in the casket girl scene the children are based on photographs of the architects' children. The girl with the Acadian family is Weiss's daughter, while the two children with the mammy are Dreyfous's son, Felix John, and Seiferth's daughter.)

In 1768 a group of prominent French Creoles led by the attorney general, Nicolas de LaFrénière, revolted against the Spanish takeover of Louisiana and drove out Governor Antonio Ulloa. General Alejandro O'Reilly, known as "Bloody" O'Reilly, came to reassert Spanish control, arrested the five ringleaders of the plot, and sent them before a firing squad on October 25, 1768, as seen in the next scene.

The remainder of this section of frieze deals with the defense of New Orleans against the British in the War of 1812. The pirate Jean Laffite offers his services to Governor Claiborne in the first scene, after having rejected overtures from the British. The Battle of New Orleans, which lasted from December 23, 1814, to January 8, 1815, is depicted in a complex and dramatic scene which extends around the corner onto the east wall and terminates with the obelisk which was erected at Chalmette to mark the site of the battle. Andrew Jackson, gesturing dramatically from his rearing horse, directs the action, while the various forces who participated in the battle prepare for combat. The architects give the following description:

> The gunboat "Carolina" commanded by Commodore Patterson in the river; land troops (Coffee's mounted riflemen, with long hair and coonskin caps, hunting shirts and belts stuck with knives and hatchets; Hinds' dragoons; Beale's creole riflemen; Plauché's and d'Acquin's battalions of free men of color; Jean and Pierre Lafitte; Dominique You, Beluche and their sharp-shooting buccaneers; bands of Choctaw braves); breastworks of cotton bales and cypress logs: the British, well groomed and outfitted under the leadership of the dignified Gen. Sir Edward Pakenham.

The section of frieze on the west wall is dedicated to the theme of Louisiana at War, personified by a rushing, sword-wielding female accompanied by a pelican. Groups from the Mexican War, the Civil War, the Spanish-American War, and World War I, depicted with historically accurate, realistic uniforms, weapons, and settings, surge from left to right. At the far right General Zachary Taylor, hero of the Mexican War, leads his troops through cacti suggesting the terrain of Mexico. Next is the first of two Civil War groups, the Washington artillery of New Orleans, with bearers of Louisiana and Confederate flags. A glimpse of the background reveals a section of the Mississippi River with chains stretched across to hinder Union navigation, and riverboats rigged for use as rams. Separated from the artillery group by the allegorical figure, there follows a Civil War infantry group under the command of General Beauregard. The Spanish-American War scene, dominated by the figure

Louisiana at War: The Civil War. West wall.

Louisiana at War: The Spanish-American War. West wall.

Louisiana at War: The Mexican War. West wall.

Louisiana at War: World War I. Northwest corner.

Louisiana at War: World War I. North wall.

of Colonel Theodore Roosevelt, is set against the backdrop of Havana harbor, with El Morro fortress and a number of battleships visible. The World War I scene is complex and involved, extending around the corner onto the north wall. The drama is described as follows:

> Modern methods of war-fare used in the great World war are shown in the other two panels of this frieze. Barbed wire cutters, a soldier with a Lewis rifle, advancing infantrymen about to draw bayonets, make this an impressive piece.
>
> A larger panel shows a dug-out covered with elephant iron with infantrymen advancing to "No-Man's Land." The "zero hour" is indicated by an officer looking at his wrist watch, and the suggested tramp of men in the winding trenches. A scolding sergeant...urging his men forward in the eloquent and picturesque language of the trenches, is portrayed.
>
> Back of these are several large camouflaged cannons. Artillery men, telephone men, and observers, each attending to their separate tasks, add realism to the picture. In the middle distance a tank is seen and in the far distance the Leviathan, with a convoy of destroyers. John A. Lejeune, commander of the marines, that Louisiana man whose leadership counted during the last war, occupies a prominent place in this picture.[25]

The frieze section on the east wall is dedicated to the opposite and complementary theme of Louisiana at Peace. Again there is an allegorical personification in the center, a seminude kneeling female with a dove of peace perched on her oustretched left hand. Behind her is a live oak tree draped with Spanish moss, and on either side are magnolias, the state flower. The figures to the left illustrate the typical agricultural activities of the state. Prominent are a pair of cotton pickers, a man cutting sugarcane, and a Cajun plowman with his team, with a row of cabbages and a basket of vegetables in the foreground. Other details in the background are less readily visible: the contour-plowed hillside, the rice field

Louisiana at Peace: Agriculture. East wall.

Louisiana at Peace: Trapping, fishing, shipping. East wall.

Frieze on east wall.

Louisiana at Peace: Children with bust of McDonogh, Gayarré writing the history of Louisiana, Audubon drawing birds, construction of levee, sculptor working on capitol, Huey Long with architects of capitol. North wall.

Louisiana at Peace: Mardi Gras. East wall.

Louisiana Law: The Louisiana Code, the Napoleonic Code, the Law of the Indies, the Black Code, the Code of Louis XIV, the United States Constitution. North wall, central section.

Louisiana Law: The lawgivers Hammurabi, Ikhnaton, Solon, and Justinian; the Louisiana Code of 1824; Napoleon. North wall.

Louisiana Law: The drafting of the United States Constitution; lawgivers Charlemagne, Julius Caesar, Solomon, and Moses. North wall.

with a sluice gate, the logging train, and the mounted overseer. To the right are activities associated with Louisiana's waterways: trapping, fishing, and shipping. The trapper stands, holding a trap, with a clothes wringer and drying rack used in the preparation of pelts. The fisherman stands in the water of a marsh, with his net and pirogue. In the background are various types of boats and ships: a flatboat or raft, a square-rigged sailing vessel, a stern-wheeler riverboat, and a modern steamer. At the far right stands a longshoreman with cotton, rice, and oil awaiting shipment on the dock. In the distance is New Orleans' haphazard skyline.

To the right of the long panel depicting the labors of Louisiana, on a slight setback, appears the state's most characteristic holiday, Mardi Gras. Masqueraders, dancing children, a carnival king, and spectators on French Quarter balconies are all crowded into this brief but charming scene.

Around the corner on the north wall are various references to the state's cultural and artistic activities: education, historiography, natural science, engineering, fine arts, and architecture. Children are shown placing a wreath before the bust of the New Orleans philanthropist John McDonogh, who dedicated his fortune to the education of the poor. Charles Gayarré, the most prominent Louisiana historian, sits writing. Behind him is the naturalist and painter John James Audubon, observing a flight of birds with palette and brush in hand. A levee-building scene follows, with a construction crane and the figure of a surveyor. The remainder deals with the capitol itself. A sculptor, possibly C. M. Dodd or Ulric Ellerhusen, is shown carving the colossal figure of Art which appears on the northwest corner of the tower. The last scene shows Huey Long and the three architects standing before the finished capitol. Weiss stands with Long, pointing toward the building, while Dreyfous, holding a blueprint, discusses a point with Seiferth. With this signature by the capitol's builders, the Louisiana at Peace section terminates.

The band of relief sculpture on the central portion of the north wall, over what was originally the law library (now the governor's office), are dedicated to the evolution of Louisiana law. Great lawgivers from ancient and medieval history are portrayed on either end: Hammurabi, Ikhnaton, Solon, and Justinian from the left and Moses, Solomon, Julius Caesar, and Charlemagne from the right. Between these rather exotic groups are scenes related more directly to the development of Louisiana's legal tradition. At the left Livingston, Lislet, and Derbigny draft the Louisiana Code of 1824. Napoleon Bonaparte stands with one of his lawyers preparing the Napoleonic Code (1801–1803), and General O'Reilly presents the Spanish Law of the Indies (1769). In the center is an allegorical personification of Louisiana with scales and fasces, symbols of justice and government, seated on a throne flanked by pelicans. To the right Bienville, with a Negro slave acompanying him, presents the Black Code of 1724, while Louis XIV and an adjutant appear behind them. Then follows the drafting of the United States Constitution (1787), with generalized

Decorative grills on front of base.

Louisiana Plants and Trees, over north entrances (above), with artist's rough model at left.

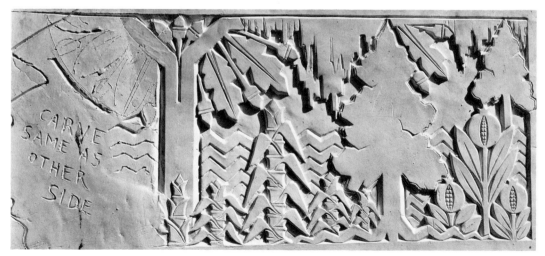

CARVE SAME AS OTHER SIDE

Decorative symbols beneath Louisiana at Peace relief.

representations of the Founding Fathers, Washington, Jefferson, Franklin, Hamilton, and Madison grouped around a table, with the Liberty Bell in the background. All of these groups are accompanied by appropriate shields or coats of arms identifying them further.

8

The Top
of the Tower

The capitol rises for sixteen floors without adornment, then proliferates into sculptured images on the upper portion of the tower beginning at the twenty-first floor level. Four large allegorical figures are carved into the corners of the tower from the twenty-second to twenty-fifth floor, with bands of ornament representing the plant and animal life of Louisiana immediately above and below them. The twenty-sixth floor level serves as a base for the temple which begins at the twenty-seventh and rises the equivalent of another seven stories.

The top of the tower presented a difficult design problem, and it was redesigned several times before a satisfactory solution was achieved. In an early rendering the tower in general has a blocky appearance, the allegorical figures are only three stories high, and the transition to the temple is a rather awkward series of setbacks. A later design shows the temple set on a higher base to achieve more verticality and more ornament to relieve the starkness. In the final solution the vertical elements are further augmented, making the setbacks less obvious and resulting in a sleeker, more coherent silhouette. The figures are increased to a height of four stories, the upper part of the temple is elongated and buttresses are added, and two floors are added to the shaft of the tower itself for increased verticality and less blockiness.

The allegorical corner figures represent "the four dominating spirits of a free and enlightened people:"[26] Law (the southwest corner), Science (southeast), Philosophy (northeast), and Art (northwest). Law personifies "justice between men and guaranteeing enjoyment in security of the fruits of industry"; Science shows "the development of invention and devices redeeming man from the serfdom of primitive labor as well as from the scourges of plagues and diseases"; Art symbolizes "the beauty in life, delighting the senses and satisfying the emotions"; and Philosophy represents "the rational analysis of human experience, applying the data

Top of shaft and tower.

Model for section of tower, floors twenty-two through twenty-five.

in all the fields of man's intellectual wanderings to the solution of life's problems."[27] The figures are described as follows:

Philosophy's head is placed in an explanatory gesture, while her head is thoughtfully bowed down. An owl is her symbol.

The Art figure . . . holds a vase, a pen, and a scroll. Her symbol is a winged horse.

The figure representing Law, bearing the fasces, or a bundle of sticks with an axe, holds the scroll and tablet in her hands. She is not shown with the sword, and she wears a firm but kindly expression, denoting the intent to guide rather than punish.

Science is indicated by a figure of forceful mien . . . with the symbols of the sun, the stars, the moon, water, and air indicated.[28]

Ellerhusen's colossal figures, like his historical frieze, are incised and angular in style. Heavily stylized, they are partly figure sculpture and partly architecture. Their wings and drapery folds are stylized into vertical parallel lines in low relief. Only the heads, shoulders, and arms emerge as anatomical features, and they too are highly generalized. The four are difficult to distinguish from each other, and their meanings are not readily apparent. The poses vary slightly in the placement of the heads

The Spirit of Philosophy. Northeast corner of tower.

The Spirit of Art. Northwest corner of tower.

The Spirit of Law. Southwest corner of tower.

The Spirit of Science. Southeast corner of tower.

Detail of Science.

and gestures of the arms. The identifying attributes held by them and by the pairs of youthful genii at their feet are difficult to see from a distance, and their meanings are ambivalent. Both Law and Art, for instance, bear scrolls.

Below, above, and between the colossal figures are reliefs representing the typical fauna and flora of Louisiana. The ornamental band surrounding the tower between the twenty-first and twenty-second floors represents the wild plants and animals. The motifs on the corners, directly below the figures, are derived from the wild vegetation of the marshes. The piers on the sides of the tower are decorated with stylized cattails, while the spandrels between them depict raccoons, mink, and crawfish representing Louisiana's wildlife. The corner ornament above the figures represents the state's cultivated crops, with motifs based on rice, corn, and cotton. The windows of the twenty-fifth floor are carved with sugarcane and magnolia motifs, while the piers at this level terminate in pelicans.

Sugarcane, pelican, magnolia motifs. Twenty-fifth-floor level.

Pelican. Twenty-fifth-floor level.

Cattails, raccoon. Twenty-first-floor level.

Sugarcane. Twenty-fifth-floor level.   Magnolia. Twenty-fifth-floor level.

Mink, crawfish. Twenty-first-floor level.

Detail of ornamental band portraying Louisiana crops at base of tower.

The severe, undecorated twenty-sixth floor is a base for Lawrie's temple. This base is meant to symbolize education, "that perfection of mind approached through the acquisition of knowledge in the realms of Art, Science, Law, and Philosophy," the foundation of the spiritual values that the temple represents. This floor, then, is a symbolic link between the allegorical figures and the temple.

The spiritual temple (now ironically occupied by a souvenir stand and refreshment vending machines) is the culmination of the capitol, both symbolically and architecturally. Weiss's prose becomes especially eloquent in describing this part of the building:

> Thus the tower rises upward and ever upward and, at its topmost reaches, culminates in a spiritual "Temple" symbolizing the noblest ideals of an inspired and enlightened people; this, in turn, being surmounted by a lantern of light sending forth the refulgent rays of faith and truth-revealed.
>
> . . . .
>
> With the approach toward more perfect knowledge man (hence, the State, since it is but the composite image of its people) develops higher and higher spiritual conceptions. So it is that the crowning motif of the building is a spiritual element — a temple adorned with the representation of the things of the heavens and of the universe without; stars and moons, and symbolic winged spheres; cloud forms and nebula. There are the urns that hold the ashes of the material life, inert, dissipated into constituent elements — symbolic of the lesser life, teaching by contrast the philosophy of the greater life. Perched upon four great pylons are the eagles of higher destiny, poised ever ready to fly to the high crags and aeries of exalted hopes and aspirations. Four pedimented portals face the four points of the compass — portals through which none may enter — opening from within, without. Thence emanate the spiritual messengers of Louisiana, bearing the lessons of experience under four dominations to guide the people of the world.
>
> Surmounting the temple, and terminating the highest reaches of the building, is a great lantern sending forth effulgent rays of light: the Light of Hope, the Light of Faith, the Light of Highest Knowledge.[29]

Pediment of temple.

Partial model of temple.

Model of temple. Detail.

Eagle. Detail of temple.

9

Memorial Hall

The interior of the capitol contrasts strongly with the exterior. While the exterior is all of gray limestone, the public spaces of the interior are profusely decorated with a multiplicity of richly colored materials. In contrast to the lightness of the exterior, both in color and apparent weight, the interior is relatively dark and heavy. Its decoration derives primarily from architectural motifs and the inherent colors and patterns of the materials, and only to a lesser degree from figurative relief carving. Over two dozen types of colored stone, much of it imported from Europe, adorn the walls and floors, while details in bronze and wood add to the overall richness of the decor.

The capitol's chief public space is the Memorial Hall, dedicated to "all of the great soldiers, statesmen, pioneers, and other benefactors, whose memory is a cherished heritage of the people of the state today."[30] It measures 35 by 120 feet in floor plan and is two stories high. Seven kinds of marble decorate its floor and walls. Statues of four historic governors of Louisiana stand in niches near the four corners. Large allegorical mural paintings cover the end walls. Surrounding the top of the wall is a band of relief sculpture in antiqued bronze repeating the historical frieze from the exterior of the building. The decorated ceiling bears coats of arms representing the nations that have ruled Louisiana. There is a considerable amount of bronzework: a large relief map of Louisiana set into the floor, decorative grilles in the walls, massive chandeliers, and the doors leading to the elevators and legislative chambers.

The floor is inlaid with squares of Siena Travertine and Yellow Travertine Antique, two types of Mount Vesuvius lava imported from Naples. The border is of four different marbles: Red Levanto, Belgian Black, Light Forest Green, and Cardiff Green. The walls of Vaurion Roche are trimmed with pilasters, niches, and door frames of Red Levanto. The bronze wall grilles, part of the ventilation system, bear stylized plant motifs.

Set into niches in the front and back walls are double-life-sized figures of four governors who led Louisiana during crucial periods of the state's history. They are Bienville, the first and most important colonial governor; William C. C. Claiborne, the first American governor; Henry Watkins

Memorial Hall.

Allen, the Confederate governor; and Francis T. Nicholls, the first modern post-Reconstruction governor. All are by different sculptors, but they do not differ significantly in style. Bienville is by Albert Rieker, who also did a number of the portraits on the Senate and House wings. Adolph A. Weinman, who did the Welfare reliefs flanking the portal, carved the figure of Claiborne. The Allen statue is by Attillio Piccirilli, whose firm did most of the capitol's bronzework. The figure of Governor Nicholls, by Isadore Konti, is that artist's sole work at the capitol.

The Abundance of the Earth is the subject of Jules Guerin's murals on the end walls. Aided by his assistant Meo Bellisio, Guerin took two months to plan these murals and five months to paint them. They were done in oil paint on canvas and shipped to Baton Rouge for installation. Both are inverted U-shaped compositions designed to fit the wall spaces around the large doorways, and their muted warmish color schemes were calculated to harmonize with the colors of the other materials of the Hall. Each mural is dominated by an eight-foot figure of an allegorical goddess standing on a low pedestal between two large urns, with figures representing the talents of the earth grouped at her feet. In the lower corners on either side of the doors are bucolic harvest scenes showing man reaping the fruits of nature's bounty. The backgrounds of both murals are generalized country landscapes.

The Goddess of Agriculture, a statuesque figure bearing a large basket of fruit on her head, is the central figure of the mural on the west wall. Completing this group are the talents of Literature, a male figure gazing at a book; Sculpture, a man displaying a sculptured figure to a young boy; and Music, a female with a harp. The two lower scenes represent agricultural abundance above and on the earth. That to the left shows a group of figures harvesting grapes and other fruits, while to the right a family pauses while harvesting grain. None of the harvest scenes involve much toil or hard labor, and the figures apparently lead an easy life.

The east wall depicts the Goddess of Knowledge, who holds a zodiac and hourglass, symbols of space and time, in her outstretched arms, Accompanying her are Engineering, a male figure with a pair of dividers; Art, a female with palette and brushes; and Philosophy, a female sitting in contemplation. The lower left scene shows figures pausing reverently for the twilight angelus in a field with their horses and sheep. The figures in the lower right scene dig potatoes, representing abundance from below the earth's surface.

A small mezzanine balcony in the north wall overlooks the Hall from the second-floor level. On the front of it is a bronze plaque bearing Huey Long's portrait which was donated by the United Confederate Veterans as a tribute to Long. Flags of the various nations which have ruled the Louisiana territory are suspended from this balcony, adding an element of brightness to a generally somber interior. These were not part of the architects' original scheme, and early photographs do not show them. The flags, from right to left in chronological order, are those of

Statue of Bienville in Memorial Hall, by Albert Rieker.

Statue of Governor William C. C. Claiborne in Memorial Hall, by Adolph A. Weinman.

Statue of Governor Henry Watkins Allen in Memorial Hall, by Attillio Piccirilli.

Statue of Governor Francis T. Nicholls in Memorial Hall, by Isadore Konti.

Mural and door at east end of Memorial Hall, leading to the House chamber.

Mural and door at west end of Memorial Hall, leading to the Senate chamber.

Ceiling of Memorial Hall.

Corner of ornate ceiling, Memorial Hall.

Urn, Memorial Hall.

Carved marble head on bench, Memorial Hall.

Flags, Memorial Hall.

Bust of P. B. S. Pinchback, the only black man to serve as Governor, added to Memorial Hall in 1976.

Castile and Leon, Bourbon France, Bourbon Spain, England, the French tricolor, the fifteen-star U.S. flag, the flag of the Republic of West Florida, the Louisiana national flag, the Confederate battle flag, the Confederate Stars and Bars, the Louisiana state flag, and the modern United States flag. The two large Sevres porcelain urns below the balcony were also not part of the original plan. They were donated in 1934 by the President of France, Albert Lebrun.

The cornices of the north and south walls of the Hall bear the same historical scenes depicted in Ellerhusen's frieze on the exterior. The positions, gestures, and expressions of the figures are the same, and the scenes are similarly composed, but this frieze is not an exact copy of that on the exterior. The figures are not as crowded together and there are more elements of setting added in the spaces between them. On the north wall, from left to right, are the sequence from the burial of De Soto to the Battle of New Orleans, an allegorical figure of Louisiana, and the sequence from Governor Claiborne's flag-raising ceremony back to La Salle's discovery of the mouth of the Mississippi. The south wall depicts the war scenes from the Mexican War to World War I, followed by the law scenes (minus the ancient lawgivers) and the peace sequence with the order of the scenes reversed.

The ceiling of the Hall is covered with stenciled oak leaf designs and bordered by shields representing the dominations of Louisiana: the Indians, Spain, Bourbon and Napoleonic France, the Confederacy, and the United States. Louis Borgo and Andrew Mackey painted the ceiling under the direction of the muralist Guerin and the architects. The color scheme of the border is dominated by the same pale, warmish hues as Guerin's murals.

10

The Bronzework

Set into the center of the floor of Memorial Hall is a large circular bronze plaque bearing a relief map of Louisiana, ten feet in diameter and weighing 3290 pounds. The names of the sixty-four parishes are inscribed in the border. The map itself shows the state's natural features and political subdivisions and bears symbols identifying the industries, products, and plant and animal life of the various regions. Stars mark the location of the capital and the parish seats, derricks indicate the oil fields, ships ply the waters of the Gulf of Mexico, and different types of wildlife, livestock, crops, and forests are shown where they live and grow.

The architect Solis Seiferth is largely responsible for the relief map.[31] He modeled it in clay at the Piccirilli studio in New York, with some technical assistance from the firm's apprentices. A railing bearing pelican motifs by Angela Gregory was placed around the relief map at a later date to protect it from the wear of people walking across it.

Other bronze details by the Piccirillis contribute significantly to the capitol's decor. Bronze grillwork of pelican and plant motifs surmounted by eagles frames the doorways inside of Lawrie's architrave. Stylized magnolia motifs in bronze decorate the windows of the Senate and House wings. The massive two-ton bronze chandeliers in Memorial Hall bear plant motifs and pelicans on their flat sides, and on their edges figures of the dominations of Louisiana similar to those carved by Lawrie on the front of the building. Similar but somewhat smaller chandeliers hang from the ceilings of the legislative chambers. The bronze doors of the main floor are all covered with pictorial panels relating to the history of Louisiana.

The doors to the three elevators facing onto Memorial Hall bear portraits of all the American governors of Louisiana from Claiborne to Long.[32] The other four pairs of doors, leading from the Hall to the Senate and House lobbies and from the lobbies into the chambers, bear depictions of historical scenes. There are fifty in all, three on each side of each individual door and two fixed in place. Each is inscribed with a caption identifying the event and its date, offering a general education in

Louisiana history. The architects prepared drawings for the scenes, which the Piccirillis transformed into relief sculpture. The panels were cast in bronze by the Cellini Company of New York and set into door frames made by the Newman Manufacturing Company of Cincinnati.

The doors facing into the Senate illustrate the evolution of Louisiana jurisprudence, while the other panels on the Senate side illustrate themes from Louisiana's colonial history. Three of the four sets of reliefs on the House side treat the history of Louisiana subsequent to the Louisiana Purchase, with the remaining set of six reliefs, those facing into the House chamber, depict the various buildings which have served as capitols.

(In the following description of the subject matter of the doors, it will be assumed that the doors are closed. The titles used will be those actually inscribed on the panels. The subjects will be mentioned in chronological order, although the scenes within each set of six are not arranged in any such order.)

The doors at the ends of Memorial Hall are framed in bronze architraves decorated with small panels symbolizing justice, music, education,

Model of relief map, Memorial Hall.

Design on bronze railing around relief map in the floor of Memorial Hall.

Bronze relief of Huey Long, beneath balcony in Memorial Hall (left); plaster model (above).

Models of bronze elevator doors depicting governors of Louisiana, Memorial Hall.

Grillwork around main portal.

Air vent, Memorial Hall.

Balcony grillwork, Memorial Hall.

Bronzework above main portal, Memorial Hall.

Door to House of Representatives.

Door to the Senate.

Detail of bronze relief on Senate door.

Three bronze doors leading from Memorial Hall to the Senate Chamber.

Door inside House chamber showing capitols of the state.

manufacturing, finance, agriculture, construction, and transportation. Above each a bronze medallion of the state seal is set into the marble. Historical scenes of special importance occupy the framed space over the doors. On the Senate side is La Salle discovering the mouth of the Mississippi River and claiming the Louisiana territory for cross and crown. This marks the beginning of Louisiana's colonial history, which is the theme of the door panels at that end of the building. The transfer of sovereignty from France to the United States, with Governor Claiborne presiding over the flag-raising ceremony in Jackson Square, is set above the doors at the House end of the Hall to set the theme for the historical scenes of Louisiana's American period on the doors of that end.

The earliest explorations of Louisiana are depicted on the doors at the west end of Memorial Hall, which lead into the Senate lobby. The Discovery of the Mississippi River by Pineda, 1519; The Drowning of Narvaez at the Mouth of the Mississippi, 1528; The Discovery of the Mississippi by De Soto, 1541; The Burial of De Soto in the Mississippi, 1542; La Salle Visits the Kappas and the Arkansas, 1682; and Iberville at the Mouth of the Mississippi, 1699, are the scenes depicted.

The reverse side of this pair of doors continues the theme of exploration and depicts the founding of early settlements in Louisiana: Bienville Meets the Ouacha and Bayou Goulas at Bayou Plaquemines, 1699; Bienville Halts the English at English Turn, 1699; The Building of Fort Maurepas by Iberville, 1700; Iberville at the Natchez Villages, 1700; The Founding of Natchitoches by St. Denis, 1714; and The Founding of New Orleans by Bienville, 1718.

The lobby side of the doors leading into the Senate chamber illustrates some highlights of Louisiana's later colonial history: The Natchez Massacre, 1727; The Arrival of the Casket Girls, 1728; The Arrival of the Acadians, 1764; The Expulsion of Ulloa, 1768; Lafrénière and the Patriots Arrested by O'Reilly, 1768; and Galvez Appeals to the Louisianians, 1779.

The Senate side of those doors shows the evolution of Louisiana's legal tradition: Bienville and the Black Code, 1724; O'Reilly Introduces the Law of the Indies, 1768; The Drafting of the Constitution of the United States; The Preparation of the Code Napoleon, 1801–1803; The Preparation of the Civil Code of Louisiana; and The Convention of 1861 in Baton Rouge.

Beneath the scene showing the United States accepting sovereignty over Louisiana, the historical sequence continues on the doors at the east end of Memorial Hall which lead into the House lobby. The emphasis of this set of panels is on the War of 1812 with scenes of The Signing of the Louisiana Purchase Treaty, 1803; The Capture of the Spanish Fort at Baton Rouge, 1810; Jean Laffite and the Baratarians; The American Flotilla Resists the British Advance, 1814; the Battle of New Orleans, January 8, 1815; and Andrew Jackson on the Battlefield at Chalmette, 1815.

The lobby side of these doors is dedicated primarily to themes of economic development; The Making of Sugar by De Boré, 1794; The Arrival

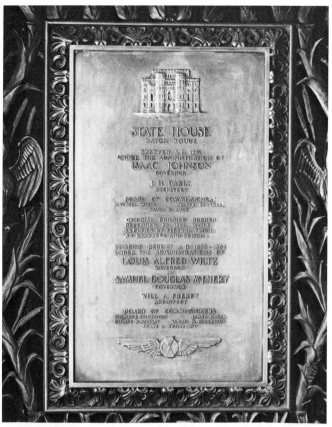

Bronze plaque commemorating old state capitol, in foyer of main portal.

Bronze plaque commemorating new state capitol, in foyer of main portal.

Plaster model of bronzework, main portal.

Bronze doorknob.

Plaster model of plaque frames.

Stairway leading to spectators' balcony in Senate chamber.

Detail of stairway.

Governor's elevator, main floor.

Model showing detail of governor's elevator.

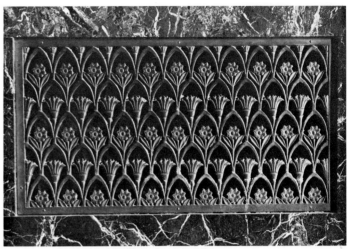

Grillwork, main floor.

Plaque marking site of Huey Long's assassination, executive corridor, main floor.

Bronze grillwork, main floor hallway.

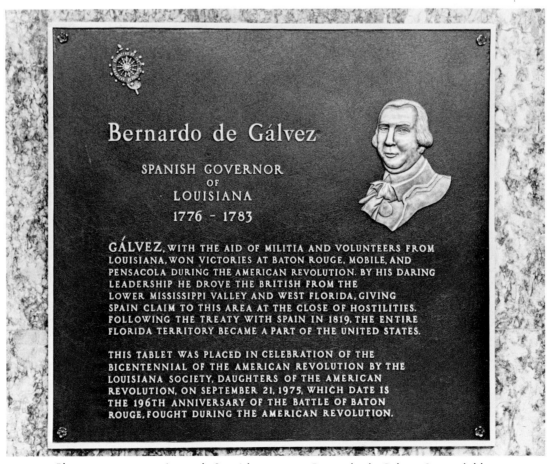

Bernardo de Gálvez

SPANISH GOVERNOR OF LOUISIANA 1776 - 1783

GÁLVEZ, WITH THE AID OF MILITIA AND VOLUNTEERS FROM LOUISIANA, WON VICTORIES AT BATON ROUGE, MOBILE, AND PENSACOLA DURING THE AMERICAN REVOLUTION. BY HIS DARING LEADERSHIP HE DROVE THE BRITISH FROM THE LOWER MISSISSIPPI VALLEY AND WEST FLORIDA, GIVING SPAIN CLAIM TO THIS AREA AT THE CLOSE OF HOSTILITIES. FOLLOWING THE TREATY WITH SPAIN IN 1819, THE ENTIRE FLORIDA TERRITORY BECAME A PART OF THE UNITED STATES.

THIS TABLET WAS PLACED IN CELEBRATION OF THE BICENTENNIAL OF THE AMERICAN REVOLUTION BY THE LOUISIANA SOCIETY, DAUGHTERS OF THE AMERICAN REVOLUTION, ON SEPTEMBER 21, 1975, WHICH DATE IS THE 196TH ANNIVERSARY OF THE BATTLE OF BATON ROUGE, FOUGHT DURING THE AMERICAN REVOLUTION.

Plaque commemorating early Spanish governor, Bernardo de Galvez, Senate lobby.

Bronzework above main portal, relief map, Memorial Hall.

Models of bronze medallions depicting state seal. The medallions differ only in border design.

Workman puts finishing touches to chandelier before its installation in Memorial Hall.

Bronzework above outside main portal (below), with model of detail (above).

of the First Steam Boat, the "New Orleans," 1812; The Reception Given to Lafayette, 1824; The Pontchartrain Railroad, 1831; Signing the Treaty with the Caddo Indians, 1835; and a view of New Orleans in 1850.

The doors leading into the House chamber illustrate scenes from the Civil War and the second half of the nineteenth century: Passing the Mississippi River Forts below New Orleans, 1862; The Battle of Berwick Bay, 1863; The Battle of Mansfield, 1864; The Battle of New Orleans for Freedom, 1874; The Mississippi River Jetties, 1878–1879; and Roosevelt's Visit to New Orleans, 1905.

The door panels facing into the House chamber show the six buildings that at one time or another had served as the capitol of Louisiana; The Cabildo, New Orleans, 1812; The State House, Donaldsonville, 1830; The State House, New Orleans, 1832–1850; The State House, Baton Rouge, 1850–1932; Shreveport: the Wartime State House, 1863–1865; and The State House of the Reconstruction Era, the St. Louis Hotel, New Orleans.

There is also a variety of railings, grills, and door knobs made of bronze.

Vent, Memorial Hall.

Grill, Senate chamber.

Model showing vent detail, Memorial Hall.

II

The Legislative Chambers

The Senate chamber, which is much larger than necessary
to accommodate the membership of that body, is divided into
thirds by two rows of piers with engaged Ionic columns, effectively
reducing the area of the Senate floor and creating wide side aisles. The
decorative motifs are all from the traditional vocabulary of classical
architecture. The rich, warmish color scheme derives from the varieties
of stone used: wall areas of Vaurion Roche Jaune and Clare ashlar, pilasters and wall panels of Violet Brocatelle marble, engaged columns and
doorways of Famoso Violet, and the floor of Roman Travertine. The
drapery in back of the rostrum, where the voting indicator is mounted,
is of red velvet. The rostrum and the desks of the individual senators,
furnishings designed by the architects, are primarily of walnut and Aus-
tralian laurel wood, with small bits of other woods used as inlays. The
ceiling is composed of deep hexagonal coffers of acoustical celotex which
conceal sources of indirect lighting.

The materials and color scheme of the Senate chamber are continued
in the Senate lobby. The walls are of Violet Brocatelle, the pilasters and
gallery stairs of Famoso Violet, the stairwells of Vaurion Roche Jaune,
and the floor of Roman Travertine bordered with inlays of the two violet
marbles.

The House chamber, accommodating many more members than the
Senate, is one large undivided space. The engaged columns which lend
the Senate its classical spirit are absent in the House. The House chamber
also contains figurative decorative motifs, which the Senate lacks. A
frieze bordering the top of the chamber consists of stylized Louisiana plant
and animal motifs, and grilles of a stylized sugarcane design ornament
the front walls. The plain wall areas are of Crazannes Anteor stone divided
by fluted pilasters of Siena Travertine. The colorful and strongly patterned
Jaune Benou marble is generously used around the doorways and the base

125

of the walls. The floor is of Roman Travertine with a border of Rouge Royal and Royal Jersey Green marbles. The furniture, like that of the Senate, is made of inlaid walnut and laurel. The wall behind the rostrum is paneled in walnut. The frame for the large voting board, inset with a clock, is carved with American eagles flanking fasces and a pair of scales.

The House lobby is decorated with several types of marble. Those used in the chamber dominate the decor: Siena Travertine for the wall surfaces and Jaune Benou for the pilasters. Rojo Alicante was used for trim around

View of Senate chamber.

Side view of columns and railing in Senate.

Border around wall of Senate chamber.

View of Senate chamber from balcony.

Ceiling, Senate chamber.

Balcony wall, Senate.

Detail of column in executive corridor near where Huey Long was slain.

Column near assassination site.

Detail of side railing, Senate chamber.

Medallions on front and back walls of Senate chamber.

Detail above center door of Senate chamber.

the openings and the base of the walls, and for the stairs leading to the gallery. The Roman Travertine floor is bordered with Rouge Royal and Rojo Alicante marble.

The executive corridor, to the rear of the first floor, connects the legislative chambers and passes in front of the original governor's suite to the north. In the middle, before the old governor's reception room, it broadens into a small vestibule with walls of Montanello marble and columns of Floredo Deep Rose. The capitals of these columns are of interest, composed of native Louisiana plants and animals, palm leaves, cattails, turtles, and alligators. The north side of this corridor was re-modeled in 1955 with wood paneling and plastic plants, and only two of the original four columns remain.

Pyrenees Black and White marble was used for the trim of the senators' reception room, while Belgian Black was used in the representatives' room at the opposite end of the hall. Both of those marbles were used in the west courtroom on the fourth floor, and Light Forest Green and Cardiff Green in the east courtroom. The stairways from the basement to the fourth floor were done in Napoleon Gray marble, while Tennessee Dark Cedar was used in the stairways from the fifth floor up. The basement corridors and the elevator corridors from the fourth floor up are of York Fossil. Victoria Pink was used in the rest rooms.

Detail of balcony railing, Senate chamber.

View of balcony and rear of Senate chamber.

Detail of House chamber door depicting capture of the Spanish fort at Baton Rouge in 1810.

Door, Senate lobby.

View of House chamber (bottom), with detail of voting panel (top).

Detail of outer door, House chamber.

View of balcony and rear of House chamber.

Detail of stairway landing, Senate lobby.

Detail of spectator railing, House chamber.

Detail of spectator railing, House chamber (left), detail of balcony railing, House chamber (right).

Detail of voting machine panel, House chamber.

Air vent in House chamber.

Detail of House chamber border.

12

The Fresco Murals

The rooms that were originally the governor's reception room, on the first floor, and the supreme court and court of appeals chambers, on the fourth floor, were decorated with mural paintings by the Louisiana artist Conrad Albrizio. The reception room was painted on all four walls with scenes of Louisiana life, and each of the courtrooms contained a scene illustrating a biblical passage related to the idea of justice. These were all done in the fresco technique, whereby the pigments are applied directly to the wall while the plaster is still wet and become physically a part of the wall as the plaster hardens. The fresco technique has not been widely used in America, and few American artists have practiced it. Albrizio's works in the Louisiana capitol are the first true frescoes to be painted in America south of Mason and Dixon's line.

The story of Albrizio's capitol murals is an unfortunate one, and only one of them exists today. By 1955, when a major cleaning and renovation of the building was undertaken, the reception room murals had cracked and Albrizio himself had estimated that their restoration would cost around $13,000. Since the murals were out of fashion at that time and apparently stood in the way of desired remodeling, those in the reception room and the court of appeals were destroyed. The surviving mural, in a good state of preservation, is covered by a curtain which can be opened. (The room is now the governor's press room.) Perhaps in compensation for the destruction of his frescoes, Albrizio was commissioned in 1955 to do a mosaic for the rear hallway of the main floor, in front of the reception room, but this mosaic was eventually installed in the supreme court building in New Orleans.

Albrizio's sketches for all the frescoes have, however, been preserved. The Anglo-American Art Museum at Louisiana State University owns the studies for the four walls of the reception room, and the studies for the

Fresco, now destroyed, originally in governor's reception room on first floor.

Sketches (above and opposite page) for reception room fresco by Albrizio.

courtroom panels are in a private collection in Baton Rouge. Also, some early photographs showing the murals in place are available.

The reception room, originally a lobby to the governor's office, twenty-one feet long and thirteen feet wide, was painted in one continuous scene all around the room. It took Albrizio and his assistant Ernest Borne five weeks to do the job. Three of the walls depict scenes of typical Louisiana life, with people working in a cotton field before a plantation house, piling bales of cotton, cutting sugarcane, and building an oil refinery. The fourth wall, which one faced upon entering the room from the hall, is more allegorical. In the center sits a figure of Louisiana accompanied by two cherubs, one bearing a horn of plenty signifying the abundance of the land, the other holding a fish representing the bounty of the sea. To the left, with the New Orleans waterfront and Jackson Square in the background, are nude allegorical figures associated with urban life: Science, standing next to a dynamo; Art, holding a small statuette; and Civic Virtue, protecting children. Figures representing the rural life are grouped to the right, with fruits and vegetables, a cow, and a turkey.[33]

The fresco in the original supreme court chamber illustrates the fifteenth verse of the 94th Psalm: "That judgment shall return unto righteousness and all the upright in heart shall follow it." Justice, a white-robed female figure, approaches with a gesture of admonishment, flanked by figures representing Fate and Law. To the right the upright in heart kneel devoutly next to a green bush, contrasted with the children of darkness who cower in fear before a barren landscape to the left.

The other courtroom fresco, destroyed during 1966–1967, was based on Deuteronomy 4:14: "And the Lord commanded me to teach you statutes and judgments that ye might do these." A white-robed female figure stands before a tree, instructing a group of people who have gathered around to hear her teachings. A shepherd stands with his flock in the middle ground, and a rainbow arches across the sky.

Albrizio also prepared a study for an end wall of Memorial Hall, the area that Jules Guerin was eventually selected to decorate. The figurative portion of the mural was limited to the area above the doorway, showing a multitude of figure groups undertaking a variety of activities. The inscription reads "Dedicated to the Eternal Spirit, Progressive Man and Civic Virtue." The areas beside the doorways were to be decorated with medallions and inscribed panels bordered by plant motifs, with American eagles at the bottom.

(The Capitol Annex, across the street from the capitol, contains four frescoes that Albrizio painted in 1938 to depict the accomplishments of the state under Governor Richard Leche. In 1940, after Leche's conviction for corruption, the House voted in favor of the destruction of the mural bearing his portrait, but it was preserved.)

13

The Grounds

The capitol grounds were carefully landscaped by Jungle Gardens, Inc., of Avery Island, Louisiana. The landscaping was a major undertaking involving the delivery and planting of over a hundred carloads of trees and plants at the site. Some larger trees were brought from Avery Island, and the camellias were transplanted from the gardens of antebellum plantations. The landscaping had to be planned in terms of how it would look when the young trees and plants reached maturity, and the architects and planners expected it to increase in beauty with age.[34]

The formal organization of the grounds in front of the capitol building is readily seen from the tower. The park, six hundred feet square, is organized around two broad walkways, each twenty feet wide, extending from the parking lot in front of the capitol southward to Boyd Avenue. A narrower path forms a circle around the main walkways, and others radiate from them to the circle. The paths are all bordered with neatly trimmed boxwood hedges. On the inside of the main walkways, bordering two sunken grassy areas, are alternating camellias and azaleas. To the outside are large evergreens—alternately junipers and arborvitae. In the center of the park, between the main avenues and the two sunken gardens, where the statue of Huey Long now stands, there is a crisscrossing arrangement of boxwood-lined walks. Three ancient live oak trees from the site of the old Boyd house were incorporated into the park, and young live oaks were planted on the east side of the park to match them. The outer perimeter of the park is planted with magnolias and azaleas. Around the park there are many smaller groupings of plants native to Louisiana, and flower beds are planned so that something will be in bloom during all seasons of the year.

The landscaping to the east of the capitol toward the Old Arsenal Museum is more irregular than the park in front, due largely to the more varied terrain. Clusters of evergreens, palms, and small flower gardens are placed around the grassy areas. The most formal element is the 60-by-115-foot rose garden, bordered by a pyracantha hedge, in front of the arsenal.

Statue and grave of Huey Long, by Charles Keck.

View of capitol grounds from the tenth floor. Huey Long's grave is in the center.

View from the capitol of the downtown Baton Rouge skyline.

The Huey Long monument in the center of the grounds in front of the capitol was erected in 1940 to mark the place where the capitol's builder is interred. It was designed by Charles Keck. The bronze figure stands facing the tower, in a relaxed pose, gesturing as if addressing an audience. A beam of light from the tower is directed at the monument at night, illuminating the statue with dramatic effect. The tall white marble base is decorated with reliefs and inscriptions referring to Mr. Long's accomplishments. A rearing winged horse on the front of the pedestal bears a ribbon with the motto Share Our Wealth. The right side shows Huey Long promoting education, distributing free schoolbooks to children, while on the left he is shown with a group of planners pointing to the capitol building, which is reproduced on the pedestal behind the statue. The back of the base bears the following inscription, with a quotation from one of Huey Long's speeches in the Senate:

HUEY PIERCE LONG 1893–1935, Governor 1928–1932, United States Senator 1932–1935. Here lies Louisiana's great son Huey Pierce Long, an unconquered friend of the poor who dreamed of the day when the wealth of the land would be spread among all the people.
"I know the hearts of the people because I have not colored my own. I know when I am right in my own conscience. I have one language. Its simplicity gains pardon for my lack of letters. Fear will not change it. Persecution will not change it. It cannot be changed while people suffer." Huey P. Long, United States Senate, March 8, 1935.

The grave monument is imposing and effective, but it must remain over-shadowed by Huey Long's grandest monument, the capitol building itself.

The Arsenal Museum and capitol grounds.

Notes

1. "Construction of Capitol Here Ends Debate Over Moving Government Seat," Baton Rouge *State Times*, May 16, 1932. This article describes the political maneuvering involved in getting the new capitol approved by the legislature. Its title refers to efforts on the part of some legislators to move the state capital to Alexandria.

2. The new capitol of Nebraska was criticized for the same reason. See Charles Harris Whitaker, "The Nebraska State Capitol," *American Architect*, CXLV (October, 1934), 9.

3. Leon C. Weiss and F. Julius Dreyfous formed their partnership in 1919. Solis Seiferth, who joined them as chief draftsman, was admitted as a partner in 1923. All had studied architecture at Tulane, with Dreyfous studying also at the University of Pennsylvania. The three worked together up to the time of World War II. Weiss died in 1946, but Dreyfous and Seiferth carried on until they dissolved the firm in 1960. Their important buildings in addition to the capitol include Charity Hospital, Lakefront Airport, and the Federal Land Bank in New Orleans, and many of the buildings on the LSU campus in Baton Rouge.

4. "The South's New Skyscraper Capitol," *Architectural Forum*, LVII (December, 1932), 523.

5. "Architects Responsible for Form and Execution of Whole Capitol Plan," Baton Rouge *State Times*, May 16, 1932.

6. "Construction Ends Debate."

7. "Louisiana Capitol Adds Monumental Building to Nation's Fine Structures," Baton Rouge *State Times*, May 16, 1932.

8. "Architects Responsible."

9. "New Capitol Represents Effort to Tell History in Enduring Materials," Baton Rouge *State Times*, May 16, 1932.

10. *Ibid.*

11. *Ibid.*

12. *Ibid.*

13. Lorado Taft, *The History of American Sculpture* (2nd ed.; New York, 1925), 587.

14. Whitaker, "The Nebraska State Capitol," 9.

15. Frank Lloyd Wright, address, "The Art and Craft of the Machine," delivered to the Chicago Arts and Crafts Society on March 6, 1901, reprinted in Edgar Kaufman and Ben Raeburn (eds.), *Frank Lloyd Wright: Writings and Buildings* (Cleveland, 1960), 55–73.

16. Walter Raymond Agard, *The New Architectural Sculpture* (New York, 1935), 37–38.

17. *Ibid.*, 36.

18. *Ibid.*, 39.

19. "Carvers Transformed Plaster Models into Stone Sculpture," Baton Rouge *State Times*, May 16, 1932.

20. Albrizio's other projects include the Capitol Annex and B'nai Israel Synagogue in Baton Rouge; the Passenger Terminal, Supreme Court, and State Office Building in New Orleans; the Courthouse in Gretna; the City National Bank in Houma; the Exposition Building at the State Fairgrounds in Shreveport; and the Waterman Steamship Company

Building in Mobile, Alabama. He also designed rugs for the Governor's Mansion. The murals in Allen Hall at Louisiana State University in Baton Rouge were done by Albrizio's students and include a portrait of him.

21. "New Capitol."

22. This warrior figure is strongly reminiscent of Hugo Lederer's Bismarck Monument in Hamburg, Germany (1905), a probable source of inspiration.

23. Agard, *The New Architectural Sculpture,* 37.

24. "New Capitol."

25. "Exterior Frieze at New Capitol is Majestic Art Work Relating in Stone Louisiana's Vivid Past," Baton Rouge *State Times,* May 16, 1932.

26. "New Capitol."

27. Weiss, Dreyfous, and Seiferth, Architects, "A Brief Description of Louisiana's New State Capitol," unpublished document.

28. "Exterior Frieze."

29. "New Capitol."

30. "Memorial Hall, Senate, House Occupy Entire Front of New Capitol," Baton Rouge *State Times,* May 16, 1932.

31. Mr. Seiferth has had a lifelong interest in maps and owns a large collection of them.

32. Two governors from the confused period of military occupation and Reconstruction after the Civil War, General George F. Shepley and Pickney B. S. Pinchback, were inadvertently left out. Other short-term governors from this period are grouped together in one panel.

33. Two additional groups, apparently representing handicrafts and fishing, were included in the sketch, of which Mr. Seiferth has a photograph, but these were eliminated in the sketch owned by the Anglo-American Museum and in the final mural.

34. "Beautiful Approach from Every Angle Is Given by Landscaping Grounds," Baton Rouge *State Times,* May 16, 1932.

PHOTO CREDITS

Solis Seiferth: 6 , 17–22, 30, 32–33, 38 (top), 39 (top), 40–42, 44–49, 52–53, 57–63, 68–69, 76–80, 81 (top and center), 82 (bottom), 83, 85–86, 89–96, 100–03, 106, 108, 109 (right), 110–11, 118 (center and bottom right), 119 (bottom right), 120 (center right), 121–22, 123 (top), 124, 130 (top left and bottom), 131–32, 137–38, 140–41.

Edgar Shore: 38 (bottom), 39 (bottom), 54, 56, 81 (bottom), 82 (top left and top right), 104–05, 109 (top and left), 112–16, 118 (top left and right, bottom left), 119 (top left and right, bottom left), 120 (top left and right, bottom), 126–29, 130 (top right), 133–36, 144–46.

Anglo-American Art Museum: 65, 70–72.

Mrs. Lawrence T. Lowrey: 66–67.

Vincent Kubly: 64.

Bibliography

Agard, Walter Raymond. *The New Architectural Sculpture.* New York, 1935.

"Architects Responsible for Form and Execution of Whole Capitol Plan," Baton Rouge *State Times,* May 16, 1932.

"Beautiful Approach from Every Angle Is Given by Landscaping of Grounds," Baton Rouge *State Times,* May 16, 1932.

"Carvers Transformed Plaster Models into Stone Sculpture." Baton Rouge *State Times,* May 16, 1932.

"Construction of Capitol Here Ends Debate over Moving Government Seat," Baton Rouge *State Times,* May 16, 1932.

"Exterior Frieze at New Capitol is Majestic Art Work Relating in Stone Louisiana's Vivid Past," Baton Rouge *State Times,* May 16, 1932.

"Louisiana's Capitol Adds Monumental Building to Nation's Fine Structures," Baton Rouge *State Times,* May 16, 1932.

"Memorial Hall, Senate, House Occupy Entire Front of New Capitol," Baton Rouge *State Times,* May 16, 1932.

"New Capitol Represents Effort to Tell History in Enduring Materials," Baton Rouge *State Times,* May 16, 1932.

"The South's New Skyscraper Capitol," *Architectural Forum,* LVII (December, 1932). 523 ff.

Taft, Lorado. *The History of American Sculpture.* 2nd ed., New York, 1925.

Weiss, Dreyfous, and Seiferth, Architects. "A Brief Description of Louisiana's New State Capitol." Unpublished document (mimeographed).

Index